Bare Feet and Buttercups

N.B.

Feast of Transfiguration occurs in August.

Trinity = 1st Sun after Pentecost

Bare Feet and Buttercups

Resources for Ordinary Time

(Trinity Sunday to the Feast of the Transfiguration)

Ruth Burgess

WILD GOOSE PUBLICATIONS

Contents of book © the individual contributors
Compilation © 2008 Ruth Burgess

First published 2008 by
Wild Goose Publications, 4th Floor, Savoy House, 140 Sauchiehall St, Glasgow G2 3DH, UK.
Wild Goose Publications is the publishing division of the Iona Community.
Scottish Charity No. SCO03794. Limited Company Reg. No. SCO96243.
www.ionabooks.com
ISBN 978-1-905010-50-9

Cover painting and internal illustration © Scott Riley

The publishers gratefully acknowledge the support of the Drummond Trust,
3 Pitt Terrace, Stirling FK8 2EY in producing this book.

A catalogue record for this book is available from the British Library.

Overseas distribution:
Australia: Willow Connection Pty Ltd, Unit 4A, 3-9 Kenneth Road, Manly Vale, NSW 2093
New Zealand: Pleroma, Higginson Street, Otane 4170, Central Hawkes Bay
Canada: Novalis/Bayard Publishing & Distribution, 10 Lower Spadina Ave., Suite 400, Toronto, Ontario M5V 2Z2

Printed by Bell & Bain, Thornliebank, Glasgow

GENERAL CONTENTS

CONTENTS IN DETAIL

Key to symbols	
✟	Prayer
✜	Biblical reflection
✄	Liturgy
((◎))	Responses
♫	Song
✍	Story
▥	Sermon
☻	Script
♥	Meditation
▦	Reflection
✗	Poem
�⟩	Creed

Key to symbols	
✟	Prayer
✢	Biblical reflection
✍	Liturgy
((○))	Responses
♫	Song
✍	Story
📖	Sermon
🎭	Script
♥	Meditation
▦	Reflection
✗	Poem
⛰	Creed

Key to symbols	
✞	Prayer
✦	Biblical reflection
Ⅾ	Liturgy
((○))	Responses
♫	Song
Ⓐ	Story
📖	Sermon
😊	Script
♥	Meditation
▦	Reflection
✗	Poem
♛	Creed

Key to symbols	
✝	Prayer
✛	Biblical reflection
∅	Liturgy
(((◉)))	Responses
♫	Song
🐾	Story
▥	Sermon
😄	Script
♥	Meditation
▥	Reflection
✗	Poem
🥾	Creed

THE FEAST OF THE TRANSFIGURATION   251

For Joan and Ralph
newly and oldly baptised
With love

INTRODUCTION

Bare Feet and Buttercups is a resource book which covers the period from Trinity Sunday to the Feast of the Transfiguration (August 6th). This period is usually referred to as Ordinary Time, or the Days after Trinity. This is the penultimate book in a series of resource books that cover the Christian calendar.★ It will be followed by a resource book called *Acorns and Archangels*, which will cover the period from the Feast of the Transfiguration to All Hallows Eve (October 31st) and will include the psalms and the prophets, gospel material after the Transfiguration, and the Acts of the Apostles and New Testament letters.

I had thought the series complete until a friend commented: 'What about all those days after Trinity?' So here they are!

This book contains material relating to Genesis and Exodus and gospel passages up to the story of the Transfiguration. There are also children's letters to the Abbot of Monkwearmouth, resources for Father's Day and for the summer, cats who like to rumba – and a talking dog.

Most of the material in this book consists of the stuff that liturgies are made of: stories, songs, responses, poems, biblical reflections, sermons and prayers.

My grateful thanks to all the contributors for the wealth of rich material I have been privileged to edit – it's been a labour of delight. It's also been the second time that one book has turned into two.

Thanks are also due, as always, to the Wild Goose Publications team: Sandra Kramer, Jane Darroch-Riley, Alex O'Neill, Tri Boi Ta and Lorna Rae Sutton, for their professionalism and support. A huge thanks is due to Neil Paynter for his attention to detail, and with whom it is a pleasure to exchange emails. Thanks also to Scott Riley for his artwork.

God of ripe plums
and meadowsweet,
thank you for summer.

Thank you for warmth
and beauty and wonder,
thank you for life.

Ruth Burgess,
April 2008

★ *Candles and Conifers: Resources for All Saints' and Advent*
Hay and Stardust: Resources for Christmas to Candlemas
Eggs and Ashes: Resources for Lent and Holy Week
Fire and Bread: Resources for Easter Day to Trinity Sunday

TRINITY SUNDAY

OPENING AND CLOSING RESPONSES FOR TRINITY SUNDAY

Year A

Gen 1:1– 2:4 or Is 40:12–17, 27–31; Ps 8; 2 Cor 13:11–13; Mt 28:16–20

Didn't you know?
Haven't you heard?
GOD OUR MAKER CARES FOR US

Didn't you know?
Haven't you heard?
JESUS OUR BROTHER WALKS WITH US

Didn't you know?
Haven't you heard?
THE HOLY SPIRIT LIVES IN US

> In peace and danger
> GOD IS WITH US

> In pain and laughter
> GOD IS WITH US

> Today and tomorrow
> GOD IS WITH US

> God is always with us
> IN JUSTICE AND IN LOVE

Year B

Is 6:1–8; Ps 29; Rom 8:12–17; Jn 3:1–17

The earth is full of glory
The earth is full of blessing
THE EARTH BELONGS TO GOD

The heavens are full of truth
The heavens are full of mystery
THE HEAVENS BELONG TO GOD

We are full of wonder
We are full of yearning
WE BELONG TO GOD

> Into your world
> SEND US

> Where people hurt
> SEND US

> Where we are needed
> SEND US

> Send us out with loving kindness
> SEND US OUT WITH HOPE AND JOY

Year C

Pro 8:1–4, 22–31; Ps 8; Rom 5:1–5; Jn 16:12–15

God the maker
God the shaper
GOD THE WISE ONE DELIGHTS IN US

Jesus the holy one
Jesus the storyteller
JESUS THE ADVENTURER DELIGHTS IN US

The Holy Spirit, the nourisher
The Holy Spirit, the questioner
THE HOLY SPIRIT THE QUICKENER DELIGHTS IN US

> Star-maker
> Earth-spinner
> God of glory
> WARM US

> Storyteller
> Justice-worker
> Jesus of Galilee
> CALL US

Truth-talker
Challenger
Holy Spirit of integrity
DRESS US

Trinity of beauty
Trinity of loving
Trinity of community
BLESS US

Ruth Burgess

A PRAYER FOR TRINITY SUNDAY

Gentle God
close to me,
hold me
in your love,
bring strength
when I feel weak,
bring courage
when I feel despair,
bring peace
when I feel afraid.

Jesus, healer,
be my companion
through my pain,
hold my hand
through suffering,
walk beside me
to steady me,
before me
to guide me,
behind me
lest I fall.

Compassionate Spirit,
alert me to your call,
inspire me to share
your passion,

your wisdom,
your justice,
to bring healing
to the world.

Elizabeth Baxter

GOD, OUR GIFTS WE LAY BEFORE YOU
Offering hymn

(Tune: Nettleton)

God, our gifts we lay before you,
gifts of hand and heart and mind;
these we offer to adore you –
may you ever in us find
willing hands for costly giving,
spirits faithful, spirits true,
shaping in our daily living
gifts of worth to honour you.

Jesus Christ, you come to greet us
stooping as a servant low –
bring the ways of God to meet us,
of his grace the fullness show.
Mystery of love's outpouring,
deep beyond our human sight,
send our earthbound spirits soaring,
re-create us in your light.

Spirit of the Son and Father,
come and fill us here and now,
as with open hearts we gather
ready to renew our vow.
Fuse the gifts our lives now offer
with the gift come from above,
seal the sacrifice we proffer
in your living deathless love.

Leith Fisher

GOD

Creator
Jesus
Holy Spirit

Star-maker
Storyteller
Breath of life

The three in one
the one times three
(I was never good
with numbers).

Enough to know
you care
you challenge
you make me holy

and you circle me
with love.

Ruth Burgess

I THINK I'VE GOT IT

Okay,
I think I've got it!

Before anything
(any thing!)
existed
you were;

and when nothing
(no thing!)
remains
you will be.

But
what I want
to know ...

Were you there
the other day
when temptation
cracked the combination
to my heart?

Will you be there
when death taps me
on the shoulder
and grins,
'Wanna go for a walk?'

And if I whisper,
'Come,
come soon,
I need you
right now.'

Will you?

Thom M Shuman

GOD OF THE STILL SMALL VOICE

God
of the still small voice,
you speak to us
when we least expect it:

WE HEAR YOUR VOICE
IN THE MOMENTS OF
CHAOS, CLUTTER AND UNCERTAINTY.

Jesus
calmer of the storms,
your very presence comforts us:

WE ARE UPHELD
BY YOUR QUIET AUTHORITY.

Spirit
counsellor,
carrier of our pain and celebrations,

we gather under your cloak of soft down
and sharp flight-feathers:

WE FEEL
THE FLUTTERINGS
OF NEW BIRTH.

Elizabeth Baxter

I BET YOU ARE NICE

Dear God,
I wish I could see you today,
I bet you are nice.
I hope you are looking after Jesus.

Lee, aged 7

A NEW SONG

Anyone could have seen the first two
just behind the fabric of the world.
The third is an unlooked-for ray of brilliance.

Power lifts over us abundantly
in sunlight, ocean, lightning;
matchless design in a bird's wing.

Only a mind sealed shut could see
and not stir to the presence
of a creating majesty.

Voices speak suddenly
with different clarity –
sing in a key nobody taught.

For those it touches
this empowerment
is undeniable as the wild wind.

But power given utterly to the task of mending,
healing, cleansing, at its own cost;
making whole what was broken;

pouring itself out endlessly
to be a light to a soul lost in the dark rocks;
spending itself as salt to fend off decay –

this is a new song,
a gift beyond imagining,
and surpassing strange.

Roddy Cowie

FATHER TO SON

I embraced God
and God embraced me in return,
father to son.

In that embrace he told me
I was a resource to be expended
in the service of his world.

When I healed,
power would come out of me.
Raising the dead would rack my body.

I would be bread
there to be broken and consumed
because his children needed it to live;

I would be salt
scattered and fouled
to hold corruption back;

I would be light
emitted to be lost
in the uncomprehending darkness;

I would be last of all,
servant of all;
I would be nothing.

I would be seed
thrown in the ground
to die.

This is the new thing that has found a footing in the world –
the spirit that expends itself without remission
as the remaker of things broken.

This is the spirit that was waiting from the first
to find the hands and feet that would empower it;
this the part of God humanity was meant to carry.

The miracle is that as its fire consumes me
it becomes such power to sweeten
God's poor soured creation.

This spirit,
loose in the world,
will not be stemmed.

Roddy Cowie

A GENDERLESS TRINITY

The Trinity is without gender: Gender belongs to created life and is not to be introduced to describe the uncreated.

Fair enough. But how are we to speak of God, when we can resort only to human languages? We have only 'he', 'she' and 'it' to call on.

These words have to be used with discrimination and in a provisional way, recognising their inadequacies.

Jesus called God 'Father'. He himself was male. So how are we to speak of the Holy Spirit? This is the point at which some say: 'You must use neutral language', as if that were the only point at which gender is introduced. But gender-free language is not available; and no question is raised about God being called Father and Jesus being male.

The Holy Spirit is also called 'he' in the bible? But in Old Testament and New Testament times, society was patriarchal. Women were treated as possessions, not equal to their menfolk. The word *adelphoi* in the New Testament can be used in two senses. It means 'brothers'. It can also convey the idea 'brothers and sisters'. But there is no equivalent case where males are tidied into a sense of sisterhood! It was men who wrote the records and they seem to have failed to question the male consciousness of their time which dominated language as it dominated life.

A different emphasis is found in the Old Testament. In the first chapter of Genesis, men and women are depicted as being given charge of life together, as God's stewards of creation and trustees. Language must reflect this.

In the second Genesis account, which focuses on the relationship to animals and to fellow human beings, it is Eve who emerges as the stronger partner. The word for wisdom, *Sophia*, is feminine. In Wisdom 7:25 we find this description: 'She is a breath of the power of God; pure emanation of the glory of the Almighty.' The word 'breath' is a translation of *ruach*, the Hebrew word for the Spirit. The Hebrew flavour of the sense of that word in Genesis, where the Spirit is depicted as moving over chaos in preparation for the work of creation, is caught accurately by John Bell, who depicts her as a mother bird extending wings and body over life as it is coming into being:

She sits like a bird, brooding on the waters,
hovering on the chaos of the world's first day;
she sighs and she sings, mothering creation,
waiting to give birth to all the Word will say.
(From Enemy of Apathy*)*

In his relationship with women Jesus lived and restored the partnership of women and men intended from the beginning of creation. His attitude, though described in traditional terms by the men who wrote the record, means that we must revise language to be as true as possible to Kingdom objectives.

So it is misleading to call the Holy Spirit 'he'. To be biblically accurate the word 'she' should be used if gender words are needed. Otherwise an all-male Trinity is assumed – the worst way of introducing gender into God!

Ian M Fraser

GOD CANNOT ABIDE SIN

You say that God cannot abide sin in his presence
and it is true, but it is not like that.

I am not what you think I am,
and I am not like you.

When you were born I gave you part of myself,
my spirit – my breath.

When my breath pulls away from me it hurts
and the pain is as intense as light.

And so I cry to you to come back,
see – this is my body being torn apart.

But if you could move with me – another self in eternity –
oh, what immeasurable joy.

I only ask you to move with me and to share the joy
that can exist in this way, and in this way alone.

You say that God cannot abide sin in his presence
and it is true, but it is not like that.

Roddy Cowie

NOT YET

(Suggested tune: Kingsfold, 8686)

'Not yet,' he said, and gently eased
her fingers from his cloak.
'Proclaim my resurrection now
demolishing death's yoke;
hold patience 'til I'm called back home,
assignment here complete:
closer I'll be than breathing,
nearer than hands and feet.'

'Not yet, I first must let my friends
test new reality;
and speak with them and eat with them
to show it's really me
who walked in journeys by their side,
who suffered and who died;
and now I live anew in love
as Bridegroom with the bride.'

'Not yet. But wait – the Spirit comes
to consecrate a feast
when bread and wine convey my life
to greatest and to least!
Then, when it's time to end earth's days
and God's own self to greet,
closer we'll be than breathing,
nearer than hands and feet.'

Ian M Fraser

GENESIS

GENESIS ONE

Break into our darkness,
formless God,
with the light
of your presence.

Split the cosmic silence
and speak in the void
of our shapeless lives.

Plant seeds of love
in barren hearts;
nourish us with your
life-bringing Spirit.

Mould us, so we become
the image of yourself,
and every facet
of our universe
displays the stamp
of your creative love.

Then help us rest
in you and see
that life is good.

Carol Dixon

GOD'S LIGHT

Four kinds of lights are lit in different areas of the worship space – e.g. a candle, an oil lamp, a torch (flashlight), an electric lamp ... plus a fifth light, which is a non-extinguishable candle.

Voice: Long, long ago, when God created human beings, he gave them all kinds of light ...

He gave them the light that comes from creation – the light of delight in the environment, the joy of nature, and the ability to use creation to sustain life and make it better. But people found that what they did also harmed creation. Some creatures became extinct and the environment became polluted. All too often, it would become dark ...

The first light is put out.

God also gave them the light of curiosity. People wondered what was over the next hill, river or sea. People wondered how things worked. So they decided to find out. They made journeys of exploration, sometimes settling in new places. They set out to find answers. The light of knowledge grew and grew. Very often, this was of great benefit and was very good. But people also discovered how to abuse the new places that they found and the people already living there. People began to use their growing knowledge for evil purposes. All too often, it would become dark ...

The second light is put out.

God also gave them the light that comes from relationships – the light of love and friendship that people could have for each other. This helped people to grow and develop and enjoy each other. This helped people celebrate joys and supported them when they were sad. But people found that too often friendships could be broken and love could turn to indifference or even to hate. All too often, it would become dark ...

The third light is put out.

As well as all these, God gave people his own light to live by. He gave them the light of his presence, the Ten Commandments and the rest of his Law: he gave them his word. People delighted in this light. They sang songs about this light. 'The Lord is my light and my salvation.' 'Your word is a lamp to guide me and a light for my path.' But often, people would turn their backs on God and ignore his word and things would go wrong. All too often, it would become dark ...

The fourth light is put out.

But then one day God decided to give people a new light. He would come among them and live as one of them. This light would give them a new way of living with him and with each other. This light would change the way people saw the world and used their knowledge. It would be a chance to begin again – a whole new start. The light was called Jesus. Some people were drawn to this light: shepherds and wise men when he was born, disciples and the poor and needy when he grew up. But by now many people had become used to living in the dark. It sometimes frightened them, sometimes confused them, and they did not always like it, but they had got used to it, and besides, who wants change? So they decided to try to put out this new light. They killed Jesus.

Someone tries to put out the fifth light (the non-extinguishable candle).

But this light would not go out. Jesus rose again.
But this did not stop people from trying.

Different people come up to try to put out the candle.

They tried ... and tried ... and tried ... again ... and again ...

And still they keep on trying.

But the light keeps on shining.
The light shines in the darkness,
and the darkness has never put it out.

David Hamflett

THE FRUIT

Such a delicate thing,
more like a ball of sun than like an apricot or a peach.
The days we'd kneel before it,
creeping in close, until it might touch my nose
its sparkle dazzling my eyes.
Surely no harm in reaching out to feel its warmth,
no harm in caressing its dimpled base,
no harm in cupping it in my palms?

It kind of just came away, like it wanted
to be plucked. That's what I said, my heart
buzzing like hummingbird wings, scouring
my mind for ways to stick it back up.

Then we looked, its glow colouring
my shaking hands. I held something
newborn. Its scent was earth
and trampled grass. I held early morning
in my hands.

Its skin split easily with my thumb, my nail wet
in its flesh. Drooling, I watched the juice bleed –
we had to hurry, had to plunge in.
Chunks came away from the stone like an antelope's
head torn from its body after the hunt.
Giggling we squeezed sap onto each other's tongue,
kissing to savour the last sharp shuddering drop.

Only then, the panic, burying the remains
like murderers, picking for hours at the strands
stuck in our teeth, washing our hands over and over,
scurrying off to the deepest groves to watch for his step.

You know the rest.

I have no regrets about what was done.
But there are mornings when I wake
on this hard savannah, dry-mouthed,
dusty-eyed, and I look down
at the cracked scoops my hands have become,
and I would cast all of you, my children,
to the jackals, just to finger its calm soft curves,
its feathery hairs, the juice weeping
through my palms again. To feel it calling,
to cradle it like a suckling son.

Rachel Mann

THE CROWN OF YOUR CREATION

Almighty God, the Lord, marvellous in majesty and power,
did you lay the foundations of the universe, nebulae and clusters,
our own world lost in its flame and mystery,
that we might be the crown of your creation, children of love?
When the morning stars sang together
did you rejoice with them to see our human birth?
Blessed be your glorious name for ever
and let the whole earth be filled with your glory.

Lord, was it of your goodwill that we were fashioned in our differences,
man in his strength and woman in her tenderness,
woman in her strength and man in his tenderness,
to make abundant life together on the face of the earth?
Blessed be your glorious name for ever
and let the whole earth be filled with your glory.

Lord, you have made us for yourself,
so that our hearts are restless until they rest in you.
Did you indeed make us restless for each other,
deep calling deep, moon pulling tide,
so that we long to make up one life, and no one lives to himself
and no one dies to himself?
Blessed be your glorious name for ever
and let the whole earth be filled with your glory.

Lord, you have made life so various.
River and rock and fertile earth,
profusion of birds among the branches and wings against the sky,
beasts wild and tame:
was it of your design that none before was like each of us,
and none shall be afterwards the same
so that we each have a particular beauty
and each a particular place in your work?
Blessed be your glorious name for ever
and let the whole earth be filled with your glory.

We should fill the earth with your glory,
men, women and children delighting in you,
making known your love in love for each other:
but we have failed you and failed our sisters and brothers.

We have used other people for our purposes,
imposing our will on them in many relationships, intimate and public,
and, getting our way, have called it love.
Forgive us, our Father.

We have been missing when young people needed help,
silent when they needed speech,
busy when they needed time,
talkative when they needed someone to listen,
lovingly interfering when they needed space.
Forgive us, our Father.

We have made family life a refuge, to protect us from the world's demand,
instead of a sure base from which to venture for right in the world.
Forgive us, our Father.

We have not shown Christ's compassion for those who have sinned
as we would not sin, or sin only in thought:
we have sat in judgement on them
instead of being found at their side,
but judgement belongs to you. Have mercy on us.

Silence

Lord, by your forgiveness, restore us to a true life
by Christ's power within us; teach us to love as he loved,
with a true regard for others and forgetfulness of self,
that, at Christ's coming, he may find faith on the earth,
and love, reflecting his.
In his name we ask it. Amen

Ian M Fraser

NOAH'S PRAYER

Lord,
I am grateful.
Really I am.
We're all safe in the ark
when everyone else is drowned.

And Lord,
I am sorry about the phoenix.
We didn't believe the stories;
we thought they were old wives' tales.
How it got hold of those pieces of flint, I don't know.
Lucky we smelt the smoke in time, eh?
Pity we couldn't save the bird.
Shem reckons it was an evolutionary adaptation to nesting in the same place
    in the desert every year.
'The fire would get rid of the parasites,' he says.
Know-all!

And Lord,
I have a rather indelicate matter to raise.
Should I mention this to you?
But you created everything
so you understand about dung.
There are piles and piles of it.
The dung beetles are in heaven —
but I'm literally up to here with it.
The others keep saying I mustn't pollute the oceans.
And that we'll need it later as organic fertiliser.
But please,
would it be OK to chuck some of it overboard?

And Lord,
they're all moaning about Japeth.
It seemed a logical division of labour at the time,
allowing specialisation, development of expertise.
I look after the mammals, Ham does the birds,
Shem takes the invertebrates
and Japeth the reptiles.
But reptiles only need feeding once a week.
He can witter on as much as he likes about constantly monitoring
    environmental conditions,

but the others reckon he's on to a cushy number.
And Shem reckons he's running out of food for the locusts
and they'll turn cannibal if they're starving.
Is he having me on, Lord?

And Lord,
we started off with two rabbits.
Now we've got fifty-four.
I thought I'd give the foxes a treat,
a bit of fresh meat.
'You can't do that!' says Madam.
'Those baby bunnies are so sweet.'
She didn't object when I fed the baby rats
to the pythons.
Is that the criterion I use to decide
who is to live and who's to die?
Cuteness?

It's enough to drive a man to drink,
it really is.

Brian Ford

LORD GOD OF ABRAHAM

(Tune: Christe sanctorum)

Lord God of Abraham, calling us to journey,
your pilgrim people, going where you lead us,
sharing your vision, wide as the sky's vastness,
help us to follow.

Lord God of Sarah, calling us to trust you,
to remain faithful through the times of silence,
give us the courage to believe your promise,
share in your action.

Lord God of Hagar, God of the afflicted,
calling the poor and those despised to serve you;
to the oppressed you come, in saving justice
with love and freedom.

Margaret Harvey

SARAH'S STORY

My name is Sarah. Wife to Abraham. Mother to Isaac. People look up to me. They give me gifts and treat me with respect. But at such cost … such cost …

I rejoiced to be married to Abraham, all those years ago in the land of my people. He was a man of vision. An adventurer. I delighted to join in his adventure. I was not like my friends who had settled into boring lives in Ur. I was a partner in my husband's quest and we both enjoyed the travelling and the uncertainty. I was relieved not to have become pregnant immediately. A child would have complicated things so. But the years went by and we travelled on and there was still no child.

Then God started to talk to Abraham. And Abraham told me what God said: How we would be the parents of a great nation, more numerous than the grains of sand by the far-off sea. But still there was no child. We were still partners in an adventure. But I would catch him looking at me with bewilderment. He would go into the emptiness of the desert and this God of his would tell him all over again that he would have a child. But God never spoke to me about it. Every month I hoped; and every month I knew myself to have failed.

So I decided one day that I had to take charge of my life before it fell apart altogether. God insisted that Abraham was going to have descendants, but didn't do anything about it: I had better organise something. So I suggested a surrogacy. I had a young slave who

was of childbearing years. Let her provide Abraham and me with a child. The baby would be ours as the slave was ours. I told Abraham that God would want us to use our initiative so that God's plan could work out, and he was easily persuaded. Hagar, that was her name, conceived immediately. And my world changed. As I watched her young body swell with the child that should have been mine I was consumed with resentment. I hated her. I am not proud of how I behaved at that time. I know I made life unbearable for her – so unbearable that at one point she actually ran away. She and the child she was carrying.

At last the child was born. Ishmael, 'God hears'. Named because Hagar had discovered that God heard her and answered her when she cried to him for help. Why did God not speak to me?

'This is my son, Ishmael. May he live in your sight,' Abraham told God. 'Yes,' said God. 'But he is not the one.' But God said nothing to me.

Then one day we had visitors. We often did. I busied myself with preparing the meal that hospitality demanded, while Abraham entertained them in the shade of a nearby tree. They moved to stand close to the tent where I worked. 'I will return to you in the spring,' one said. 'I will come to see the son that Sarah will have by then.' I laughed. I laughed so that I would not cry at the cruelty of it. My periods had stopped. I was old. To talk in such a way was insensitive and unworthy of a guest at our tent. The man who had spoken heard my laughter. 'Why does Sarah laugh?' he asked. I was embarrassed, and beginning to be afraid at the strangeness of this visitor. 'I didn't laugh,' I called out hastily, 'you are mistaken.' 'Yes, you *did* laugh,' he said. His voice was gentle and understanding and full of humour. I carried on with the cooking, feeling bewildered. Later, I remembered his voice. For I did have a child. Isaac, my child of laughter. It was an uncomfortable pregnancy and a hard birth. But I was full of joy. We agreed that the visitor had been God's messenger. I remembered how he had placed himself where I would hear and be heard. Now I knew God listened to me as well as to Abraham.

But long years of inadequacy don't vanish overnight, or even over nine months, I discovered. I could not bear to have Ishmael near Isaac. Isaac loved to play with him. But I remembered that Ishmael was the first-born. I remembered Hagar's glowing pregnancy and watched her delight in playing with the children. So I made Abraham send them away.

We are a family now. But there is no longer the easiness of partnership Abraham and I used to have. I look at him and wonder if he thinks of his first-born. And of Hagar. And what he thinks of me. And what God thinks.

Margaret Harvey

HAGAR'S STORY

My name is Hagar. I am Egyptian, born in the plains of the great River Nile. But I remember little of my home country. For I was just a small child when I was sold to Abraham, a traveller from the east. As I grew older and learnt the ways of his household he gave me to Sarah, his wife, to be her slave. I journeyed with them, north to the land called Canaan. For ten years I served her. I was happy. Abraham I feared, for he was a great man, the leader of his tribe, with the strange, distant eyes of the traveller. But Sarah I loved. She was beautiful. As she grew older her beauty grew greater. And she was a gentle mistress. We grew very close. She talked to me, and I grieved for her and with her as the years passed and there was no child. How she longed for a child. The longing filled her life. I stayed close as she wept each month. And wept for her as I watched her pick up hope again and wear it defiantly.

Then one day she called me into her tent. Her face was determined and resolute. She told me that she and Abraham had found a solution. She explained that I could give them the longed-for child. I was filled with love and pity. I was glad, I said, that I could do this thing. I would show my love for my mistress and bear her child. She took me by the hand and led me to Abraham. And left me.

I conceived immediately, but instead of it being an occasion for joy it put a distance between me and my mistress and between Abraham and his wife. I thought I saw her look at me with envy and I resented that. She had given me away – I had grown to believe I was her friend. I had almost forgotten that I was a slave. But she had given me away as if I were a thing. But I was pregnant. I had done what she could never do. Her love for me changed to bitterness and hatred. Abraham kept away from us both. There was no help there.

One day she struck me and I became afraid for my child, as well as for myself. I could never think of the child I carried as belonging to her. It was mine. My responsibility. My joy. So I ran away.

And my world changed. I wept as I went, until my eyes were swollen and I could hardly see where I was going. I didn't see the man waiting by the spring until I was almost upon him. I was afraid, for he was a stranger and I was alone. But he spoke to me: 'Hagar' – how did he know my name? 'Hagar, slave girl of Sarah,' he said, 'where have you come from and where are you going?' 'I am running away,' I said. I felt like a little child. Then he started to talk to me about my baby. He called him Ishmael, as if it had been long agreed as his name, although I had not thought of it. He told me strange things of a great future for this child I carried. 'Go back to Sarah,' he said. So I did.

There had not been time for me to be missed. Nothing had changed. Yet everything had changed for me. I'm not sure how I knew, but I *did* know, that the stranger had been the angel of Yahweh, the God of my master, Abraham. I gave him my own special name. I called him 'The Seeing God', because he had seen me – not just glanced my way but *really* seen me. Me, a slave.

My child was born and I insisted he be called Ishmael. Sarah and Abraham tried to act as if the boy was theirs. But somehow it didn't work. I looked after him. He was my child. He was a beautiful child and grew alert and strong. Then the impossible happened – Sarah herself conceived. In her joy she became again the loving mistress that I used to know. But I trod warily now, no longer at ease with her. I was right to do so. For when the child was born she turned against my Ishmael. Now I was not running away. Instead I was told to go. She could not bear the thought that they should grow up together. This child that I had borne for her – she could not stand to look at him. So we went.

For a time we barely survived. It was hard bringing up a child by myself. I moved from one encampment to another, finding shelter and food wherever I could. We did survive. Ishmael is grown now. A strong man. A skilled hunter. I found him a wife who came from Egypt as I did. I never saw Sarah and Abraham or Isaac again. Despite the sadness of that time, I do not regret that I grew up in their household. How else would I have learnt of Yahweh, my Seeing God? In all the years since, he has been with me. He has cared for Ishmael, a father even greater than Abraham. I no longer hate Sarah. I hope she has been found by my Seeing God, too.

Margaret Harvey

JACOB'S LUZ BECOMES HIS BETHEL

(Genesis 28)

This sermon was given at an agape service at the end of a week on Iona.

He was on a sort of pilgrimage, Jacob.

A sort of 'pilgrimage through life':
a journey to an uncertain new home
in the hope of finding work and,
under pressure from his father, Isaac,
a wife:

The sort of uncertain and vulnerable pilgrimage through life
that most of us are on,
most of the time.

And he found himself in a very ordinary place, Jacob:
a shelter for the night on a rock in a town called Luz.
The sort of place you just pitch your tent, then pass on through
without really giving it a second look.
The sort of place where we all spend our lives,
most of the time.

But ordinary places can become extraordinary
if the eyes of our hearts are opened to see them that way.

And ordinary journeys through life can be transformed wondrously,
anywhere,
by encounters with the Divine.

So in the dark of a dreary night
on a campsite in humdrum Luz
the seeker Jacob met God in a dream,
and God promised him a certain future;
a blessed future;
a future full of promises which far exceeded any aims and intentions
that young man had;
a future which only his father Isaac might have imagined
or hoped for his son.

As Jacob woke up from this life-transforming dream
the eyes of his heart were opened
to see the place he was in
in a very new way.

'Surely God is in this place – and I did not know it!' he said, amazed.

'This is an awesome place,' he said, astonished. 'Surely it is the House of God – it's a gate that leads to heaven!'

And he renamed Luz, Bethel, which means 'House of God'.

And Bethel has ever since been known as a holy place
to many religious traditions
and many hopeful travellers-through-life ...

We find ourselves together here tonight
in a place which has, for longer than anyone can remember,
been thought of as holy

(though a place of hard work and honest toil – an everyday place – for
those who have made this exposed slice of rock their home).

And we have offered each other 'peace'
for our onward journeys:
maybe journeys like Jacob's –
pilgrimages through life,
hoping and dreaming.

So we celebrate tonight
that our Luz can become our Bethel,
if we open the eyes of our hearts
to the possibility
of the Divine breaking into our everyday lives.

And we can leave this holy place
(whether tomorrow or on another day)
in the firm faith
that any place
and every place to which we travel
can be a house we share with God
can be a gate which opens us to heaven.

John Davies

NO CHANGING HISTORY

Genesis 37

He was a dreamer,
our Joseph.
Dreams are strange things sometimes,
and if he'd been older and wiser
he might have kept his dreams to himself.

Nobody wants a spoilt baby brother –
and a spoilt teenager is even worse.
Mind you,
dad giving him that long robe
hadn't helped much, had it?
Though at least he'd seen through
the sun, moon and stars routine
and had told Joseph to mind his mouth.

We got our chance in Dothan
when Joseph came out alone to find us.
Most of us would have happily killed him
but Reuben wouldn't have it,
and his word goes.

We stuck Joseph down a well instead.
It was a dry one
and it wasn't that deep,
but deep enough for him not to climb out on his own.

As chance would have it
some traders came along the path
and Judah suggested selling Joseph as a slave.

We did OK.
Twenty pieces of silver.
And it was 'Goodbye, dreamer.
Have an interesting life!'

We showed dad Joseph's robe,
we'd smeared it with animal blood,
and dad drew his own conclusions.

Dad's never really got over it,
but there's no way we can tell him
what really happened.
I'm ashamed now of what we did,
but there's no changing history,
is there?

Ruth Burgess

EXODUS

HEAR MY CRIES, MY PRAYERS

Loving God,
I can't find the right words for prayers.
I can't address you like a public meeting, as in church.
If I try to speak to you as a friend, awe overwhelms me –
for you are the Creator of this vast universe;
my words dry up:
so I give thanks for the story of the exodus
which tells that you hear cries, not just prayers.

Hear the cries of the oppressed.
Hear the cries of the hungry.
Hear the cries of the poor.
Hear my cries, my prayers.
I ask this in Christ's name.
Amen

Ian M Fraser

HOLY GROUND

'Take off your shoes,'
God said
to a puzzled Moses
staring at a bush
on fire for ever.

'For you're standing on holy ground,'
God said
to an attentive Moses
wondering at
a bush that could speak for God.

'Me? Shoes?'
Moses said
to the voice that spoke
amazingly,
and said, 'I Am for you.'

'Holy ground?'
Moses said
to the voice that called him forth,

the God who now believed
he'd found his man.

'I Am will send you,'
said God
to a stuttering failure,
who only wanted
to be excused the call.

'Holy ground?'
said Moses ...
'That's enough for me!'
picking up his shoes
in case he needed them for the journey.

Tom Gordon

THE BUSHES ARE BURNING

A meditation

Moses was minding the flock of his father-in-law, Jethro – you could say he was minding his own business, doing the ordinary things of every day. Minding the sheep on the mountainside, when he saw, to his amazement, a bush which was burning but was not consumed. His curiosity was aroused. 'I must go and see this wonderful sight. Why does the bush not burn away?'

And when the Lord saw that Moses turned aside to look, he called his name and said: 'Take off your shoes, for the place where you are standing is holy ground.' And Moses knew that it was the voice of God ...

Take off your shoes.
Hear the Lord calling you by name and saying,
'Take off your shoes,
for the ground you stand on is holy.'

As you walk through your ordinary days, minding your own business,
doing what you know well,
prepare to be surprised – for all around you the bushes are burning.
You only have to take time to turn aside to look,
and listen for the voice of God:

> In the dawn of the new day and the warmth of the sunshine,
> the bush is burning.

In the beauty of the moonlight and the shining of the stars,
the bush is burning.
In the beauty of the season and of all created things,
the bush is burning.
In the people you meet and the work of this day,
the bush is burning.
In the peace of the evening and the stillness of the night,
the bush is burning.

But you must turn aside to see.
For only then will you
hear the Lord calling you by name and saying,
'Take off your shoes,
for the ground you stand on is holy ground.'
So take off your shoes and reverence that which is before you.
And in the middle of your ordinary days,
when you are minding your own business,
turn aside to look
and know
you are standing on holy ground.

Lynda Wright

BEHOLD THE LAMB OF GOD
(Exodus 12:1–14)

How do we tell this bizarre story
of healthy young creatures slaughtered,
blood spread on doorposts,
every mother's first-born killed?

Was there no easier way to set your people free?

How do we end the tyranny of oppression
without the spiral
of violence on violence
liberation sought through terror?

Is there no easier way to set your people free?

How do we learn a new way of living
which replaces hatred with respect

seeks truth with forgiveness,
pursues peace with justice?

Is there a better way to set your people free?

Look,
the Lamb of God,
sharing our pain on the cross,
blood turned to new wine,
death transformed by life.

Is this your way to set your people free?

Jan Berry

THE OFFICIAL STATEMENT

Actually, they went with our blessing.
We are always pleased when economic migrants
choose to return to their country of origin voluntarily.
They were a burden on our economy,
a drain on our resources,
and were taking jobs, such as brick-making,
from our own people.

The face-to-face negotiations
between Pharaoh and the Israelite leader Moses
involved some hard bargaining.
But the talks ended
with a degree of mutual respect and cordial understanding
and a clear road map of the way forward.

It is perhaps relevant to remember that this is the 'silly season'.
At other times of the year
neither an unusually large number of frogs
nor a red tinge to the waters of the Nile
would have been headline news.
Both phenomena are being investigated by government scientists
and will doubtless prove to have perfectly rational explanations.
Any suggestion that they are in any way connected
with the departure of our Israelite guests
is, of course, fanciful nonsense.

And plagues of locusts
and freak weather conditions,
although unusual,
are certainly
not miraculous.

The recent epidemic,
although obviously highly contagious and virulent,
was rapidly brought under control
by the quarantine restrictions and public health measures,
applied with great efficiency by government medical teams.

The chariot escort for our departing friends
is completely normal procedure
in such circumstances;
and the tragic incident at the Red Sea,
and the resultant loss of life,
is to be greatly regretted –
and his divine majesty extends his heartfelt sympathy
to the relatives of the deceased.
A comprehensive enquiry has been launched,
and a full report will be published
when it has been completed.
Preliminary findings indicate
that the incident was due solely
to the incompetence of the commander,
who would have been severely punished,
had he survived.

Current reports indicate that
the rather pathetic little band of Israelites are, at present,
wandering aimlessly in the desert region near Sinai.
In due course they will undoubtedly disappear completely
from the pages of history.

Brian Ford

BREADMAKING GOD

(Exodus 16:2–15)

Breadmaking God,
providing food for your children
with an abundance that surpasses our hopes,
we praise you.

GOD, MAKER AND BREAKER OF BREAD,
FEED AND NOURISH US WITH YOUR LOVE.

Breadmaking God,
working with those who sweat and struggle
to provide food and nourishment for the hungry,
bring justice to your world.

GOD, MAKER AND BREAKER OF BREAD,
FEED AND NOURISH US WITH YOUR LOVE.

Breadmaking God,
hearing our greedy clamour for more,
our desire for possessions surplus to our needs,
forgive us.

GOD, MAKER AND BREAKER OF BREAD,
FEED AND NOURISH US WITH YOUR LOVE.

Breadmaking God,
offering us the bread of life,
mysterious in its brokenness,
feed us.

GOD, MAKER AND BREAKER OF BREAD,
FEED AND NOURISH US WITH YOUR LOVE.

Jan Berry

THE MANNA JAR

Usually it's stuck up on the top shelf of the bookcase next to my desk, but lately, I have been keeping my 'manna jar' close by my side.

Well, actually it's not a jar, but a Sainsbury's Assorted Biscuits tin from England. And instead of being filled with delicious treats (which are long gone!), it is filled with 'manna', bread of heaven – all those gifts from God that remind me that I am God's beloved child.

There are cards from families thanking me for funerals, weddings or baptisms which I have done; there are crayoned notes from children who now have children of their own; there is a picture of my mother, taken when she was much younger; there are emails from friends and colleagues; there is a ribbon which wrapped chocolate that a dear friend brought me back from France; there is a stone from Lindisfarne; some sand from Martyrs' Bay at Iona; a rock from Omaha Beach; a pressed flower from Taizé.

They are reminders of places where God has led me, of people with whom God has graced me, of all the gifts God has poured out upon me over the years. They are 'outward and visible signs' of that invisible and spiritual bread of life God gives to us each and every day, if we only take notice.

When I am spinning and whirling from a life of stress, I open my manna jar and breathe in the sweet aroma of the Spirit's healing presence, and it seems my hyperventilating soul begins to calm.

When the demands of ministry have stripped me bare, I touch the words, the paper, the stones – all those inanimate objects that put sinew and muscle back onto my dried bones.

When I hunger for a friend, an affirmation, a reminder that God loves me and cares for me, I feast upon these tender sweets, and my emptiness is filled to overflowing, my broken spirit is made whole.

And I put the lid back on my manna jar, and continue on through the wilderness.

Thom M Shuman

WITH UNVEILED FACES

'When Moses went down the mountain, his face was shining because he had been speaking with the Lord.' (Exodus 34:29)

Light up
my life, loving Lord:
let me reflect the radiance
of your love on those around me.

Burn within
my being, until I am aglow
with your grace, O God.

Reach beyond
my earthbound existence
into the heart and soul of each community
with whom I come into contact.

Transform me
with your glory,
so all will see and know
that you are God.

Carol Dixon

NOT COUNTING

(Exodus 12:37; 15:20)

They were tired:
tired of cajoling the children,
tired of packing and unpacking and packing,
tired of carrying the food and the baking pans,
tired of walking.

I didn't think that they had any energy left,
but they did.

They were anxious:
anxious about their enemies,
anxious about their older ones and their little ones,
anxious about the future,
anxious about the unknown.

I didn't think that they could let go of their anxieties, even for a moment,
but they could.

It was a risk.
I thought I might be on my own,
that no one would join me,
that I'd look a fool.

I wondered if, after my brother's long song,
my sisters would have had enough of singing,
but they hadn't.

And so I sang for them,
and I sang with them
and I danced,
and I played my tambourine.

And the dry ground was beaten firm
by the feet of six hundred thousand women dancing,
not counting men
and sheep and goats and cattle,
and children.

Ruth Burgess

AMAZED

He stretched out his staff and the waters parted!
I thought: What a man, this Moses,
as I stood and watched –
amazed.

God, give me boldness to trust you now,
that I might know you working through me
and be amazed again.

He threw a stone from a sling and a giant was defeated.
I thought: What a kid, this David,
as I stood and watched –
amazed.

God, give me strength and purpose as I go forward now,
that I might smite the giants of fear and injustice
and be amazed again.

She saved her people from their death with her courage and devotion.
I thought: What a woman, this Esther,
as I stood and watched –
amazed.

God, give me love and passion as I try to stand for what is right,
that I might find a courage that comes from you alone
and be amazed again.

He kept his faith in a greater God even in the face of disasters.
I thought: What a guy, this Job,
as I stood and watched –
amazed.

God, help me acknowledge you as wise and great,
that I might find true meaning for my life in you
and be amazed again –
and again,
and again ...

Tom Gordon

FRIENDS AND FAMILY OF JESUS

CATCHING PEOPLE

Peter: I'm a fisherman,
            as was my father and grandfather
            and all the men in the family as far back as we can go.
            It's what we know,
            it's in my blood.

            So a night like last night,
            bringing in those nets forty times
            without a single fish, is embarrassing –
            as well as leaving me skint.

            Now I'm not one for 'religious talk' –
            I leave that to the priest –
            but give me a job needing doing, and I'm your man –
            I like to get my hands dirty.

            But that catch today ...
            heaving those nets,
            barely staying afloat –
            it hit me there and then.
            Something made me get down on my knees –
            it was almost as if God was sitting there in my boat.

Jesus: There's nothing to be afraid of.
            Come with me and help me with my work:
            but we won't be looking for fish.

Peter: So – this morning I've left two nets full of fish
            to Jesse and Jacob in the village
            and here I am,
            travelling on the road with the teacher,
            God only knows where.
            Catching people, he says.

Alison Adam

COME AND SEE (ANDREW REMEMBERS)

(John 1:38)

I followed him. It was not far away.
Ordinary. In fact, rather frugal.
And yet, looking back to that fateful day,
his presence gave that house an almost regal air I sensed
but little understood.
The table well-wrought, a few simple chairs.
I only learned later his skill with wood
and wondered if lifeless timber bears
his mark as much as I do. My life's core
changed that day. There were other rooms but none so
clearly etched in my memory. That door
led to another world. I had to go
on following him. Left my nets behind.
He called us to fishing of a different kind.

Mary Hanrahan

'AND SHE AROSE AND SERVED HIM'

(Matthew 8:15)

I organise a feminist theology circle in Tokyo. We look at bible stories and characters and try to imagine the other stories which may have existed but weren't written down.

Today mother was worse than usual. Her anger had a grimmer, more scathing edge. Her eyes red with fever and tension, she groaned as the silence moved with boisterous friendly voices. People came in, a lot of people. Then my husband's voice, a little higher than usual.

'Miriam, *Miriam*, we have guests.'

Peter's head appeared between the heavy curtains that divide the main room from our small back room.

'Put a fire on and fry some fish, get the bread and the oil. The teacher has come to our house!'

I can see that I am supposed to be delighted, but since Peter took up with this prophet and became a 'fisher of men' (like that's something we need in this house!) and not a fisher of fish, it has been a regular struggle for me to put food on the table for our family and also care for mother.

I tell Peter, 'Mother is very ill, worse than usual. I will set the fire, but you will have to do the rest yourself.'

He looks at my face, as cold as my mother's is hot, and does not argue. I gather the wood and try to get a fire going. Our visitors huddle on the floor in a circle, rubbing their hands, looking like little children. I see Peter's younger brother, Andrew, I recognise our local tax collector – and it seems like all the poor of the town. Women too. One, whom I recognise as Mark's wife, Rachel, gets up to help me.

'Please sit,' I say. 'There is very little to do. We have very little to offer.'

Rachel comes and kneels beside me and helps me light the fire.

I am guessing that the one Peter is falling all over is the prophet, though he is as scruffy as the rest. Looks OK though, a bit thin, nice smile. Wish he could sort out our family problems like all this other stuff he is supposed to have done. I can't stop a smile. Now *that* would make a believer of me.

Mother shouts from the back room. I show Rachel where the food is.

I sit beside mother. Her body is burning. The curtain moves, and the prophet comes in. He sits and talks with us. Mother is not having it but he seems fine with that. 'Anger and fear and frustration,' he is saying. He touches her brow and holds her hand. I don't know what he is going on about, but I see her turn to him. Heat is going from her; she moves herself around for the first time in weeks.

Mother is getting better. I watch her body soften as he strokes her head. I hear her ask him if he would like something to drink. Then I watch as mother goes to the water jug and starts to serve not just him but – going out into the other room – all of them. He joins the circle again, quieter. He is smiling to himself. I watch, still in a spell, as he takes mother and sits her in his seat, then goes over to where Rachel is doing her best to pre-pare a meal from very little. A sudden silence falls.

'Rabbi,' says Peter, 'this is not your place.' He is glaring at me.

The Rabbi places the bread at mother's feet and pushes Peter gently by the shoulders to go and sit beside her.

'Peter, you need to learn, and I do too, that our place is to serve.'

Rachel motions me to come sit and share in the meal.

I try not to smile too much. This is a prophet I could take to.

Alison Gray

HE'S MY SON

(Mark 3:31)

He's my son
and he hurts me so.
What else can I do for him?
I've fed him, clothed him,
listened to him.
And believed in him.

I've protected him as best I can.
Guided him
supported him in his work
encouraged him to find love
even when everyone, even his followers,
frowned on such a thing.

They were frightened of losing him.

How could they?
*You are all my brothers, and my sisters
and my mother.*

Hurtful, but truthful
stinging words of love.

I caught a woman's eye in the crowd.
Another Mary, with a reputation amongst the men.
But I don't care; she saw my pain – had seen much
pain of her own.
And she smiled at me, softening his words.
Her look made me understand them.
And the look she gave my son
helped me understand something else too.

I can dream, can't I?

Alma Fritchley

JAMES

My lot were a typical village family.
Dad was the local carpenter, builder, whatever.
He was called Joe, not that us kids ever called him that, although mum did.
We just called him 'Dad'.
Mum was, well, mum was just mum.
She was called Mary.
Again, us kids never called her that,
although we heard dad call her that often enough from his workshop
when he was wanting his elevenses
or wondering when he would get his lunch.
We just called her 'Mum'.
Then there were all us kids, all higgledy-piggledy together in our house.

I was one of the younger ones.
Never mind my sisters, it was my big brother I always looked up to.
He was bigger than me.
A lot bigger.
He could always beat me when we wrestled or ran or whatever –
when he could get away from helping out in dad's workshop, that is.
I thought he could do anything.
I thought he was so clever.
I thought he was God.
Well, you do, don't you,
like all little brothers who think their big brother is their greatest hero.
Mum thought he was God, too.
But, then, that's mothers and their eldest sons for you.

Well, we grew up, as kids do.
Dad died, mum cried.
But it was a lovely funeral – all the neighbours came.
My brother took over dad's business.
Business as usual.
And, although grown, I still looked up to him.

Then there was that day when he simply downed tools and went off.
Mum cried again.
The neighbours all thought it was a right rum do.
'He should stay put.'
'He's got his family to provide for.'
'He's got responsibilities.'
And there were dark mutterings about our cousin Johnny.

Bit of an oddball, our Johnny.
Came to a sticky end.
The neighbours thought that he was leading my brother astray.
We heard about some of his new pals.
Fishermen are okay, I suppose, although they always stink of fish.
But a tax collector – nothing but a Roman lackey!
And a Zealot – a religious bigot who wants to kill in the name of God!
Well, I ask you!
He started going on about God and stuff.
We all thought he was mad.

Mum took us all off to try and bring him home.
We could all look after him, try and sort him out.
And if not, well, we could just hide him away somewhere.
Didn't work, though.
He just stayed with his pals.
Didn't seem to want us any more.
Anyway, mum and my brothers and sisters went off home.
I thought I'd hang around a bit, see what was up, all that sort of thing.
Because, for all that, I still looked up to him.

So off I went, traipsing round the place along with all the others.
I got to like them – they were not such a bad lot after all, apart from one.
Those crowds!
They couldn't get enough of him.
And I tell you, the things I heard, stories like he told me when we were kids!
And the sights I've seen!
Sick folk made better!
And that seaside lunch!

He never married.
Did I tell you that? No?
Well, there were plenty of nice women to choose from.
There was that Martha – she'd have seen him well-fed!
There was her sister, Mary – bit of a drip, but my brother had a soft spot for her.
And there were others, like that other Mary – bit of a racy past she had!
Anyway, as I said, off we went all round the place.
He'd talk to anybody and everybody,
especially to all those folk others wouldn't give the time of day.
You know, poor folk, lepers and such.
I looked up to him more and more.

Then we all went off to Jerusalem – the Big Smoke.

We thought it was great – the crowds waving and all!
Even mum came – although the others didn't.
Then it all went sour.
We had a grand old supper together – the last one, as it turned out.
That pal of his, you know, the one I was none too keen on,
well, he turned him over to the authorities.
Regular little Judas he turned out to be!
Mind you, we were not much better.
Some friends we turned out to be! Some brother!
We all ran off, left him in the lurch.
The bigwigs had some sort of confab and turned him over to the Romans.
They had some sort of show trial
then strung him up with a couple of other poor devils.
Mum was there – said later it was a terrible sight.
He died, mum cried.
Just like with dad.

None of us went to the funeral.
Just a couple of blokes, Joe and Nick.
They were toffs, so it didn't matter to them what others thought.
Decent men. Good of them to take care of things.

Then there was that amazing thing – the bit you won't believe.
My brother came back!
There he was, dead and buried, cold in his grave.
Three days later, we were all together and there he was –
my brother in the middle of us.
Hard to believe, I mean none of us did at first.
But there you go.
He was alive!

Well, I've gone on long enough about my big brother.
I'm one of the leaders of his movement now.
He's still bigger than me.
A lot bigger.
I still look up to him.
I remember saying to mum, just after my brother came back from the dead,
'You know, Mum, when he and I were kids, I thought he was God.
Now I know he is.'
Mum just smiled that secret little smile of hers,
and said that she'd known that all along.

David Hamflett

ASLEEP IN THE STORM

(Mark 4:35ff)

Jesus!
For God's sake, wake up!
Another wave like that last one
and we'll have had it!
How can you sleep
so peacefully?
Shipwreck stares us in the face!
Our sail can't hold out much longer,
then the currents will finish us off.

My shoulders are aching
trying to control this tiller;
my hands are sore
struggling with these ropes –
while you sleep!

See those rocks?
It's taking us
right towards them.
There's some good lads
died on them –
it'll soon be us too.
Come on, Jesus!
Get baling!
Wake
up!

Ian Cowie

WALKING ON WATER

(Matthew 14)

They came to me anxiously and officiously: 'Send them away now – we can't feed them – they have no food.'

What could I do? The air was thick with tiredness. It had been a long day.

Then I saw a young lad, standing by Andrew. 'Here,' he said, 'they can have mine.'

He held out his bundle of bread rolls and dried fish, with no doubt that it would be valued and used.

So I took it, and the people were fed, the disciples walking – then running – round in wonder. The boy walked away, carrying a basket filled with food for his family, his face alive with delight. I wanted to keep looking at that face, to relish the effects of a child's faith. So I persuaded the disciples to set out while I spoke with the last stragglers of the crowd. There were plenty of people with boats, I could easily follow later.

A little way up the hill there was a scrubby outcrop with a small, wind-stunted tree. I sat, leaning against the firm trunk, and exhaustion settled around me like a cloak. So many people, uncertain and confused like shepherd-less sheep on a mountain. I bowed under the weight of their need and my loneliness. Then, like a hand on my shoulder, I knew that my Father felt it too. I spread before him the impossible vastness of need. The night wore on, and I sensed the assurance that he had it in hand, and I was filled with wonder and hope. I remembered the boy's face, laughing with sudden joy.

The wind had built up, blowing in from the sea. I got up and walked down to the water's edge, leaning into the force of the wind. I realised I could still see the boat, held almost stationary, like a gull trying to fly into a gale. And I forgot to think, to consider implications – still held by the child's delight, I ran to them across the sea.

The wind carried their voices. 'Look! A ghost!' 'No,' I called with laughter. 'Don't be afraid! It's me!' 'Is it really you? Can I come to you?!' shouted Peter. He leapt over the side of the boat, and the child's delight was full in his face, so that for a long moment we stood and laughed at one another. Then the wind caught him and his delight was replaced by fear and a sudden realisation of the dark depths, and he cried out in terror. I loved this large and impetuous man. I reached out to him. As he clasped my hand joy returned. Together we climbed into the boat and our laughter danced till all were caught in its net. And the wind ceased.

Margaret Harvey

STORIES AND SAYINGS
OF JESUS

THE EYE OF THE NEEDLE

(Tune: Four Maries)

'It's hard to enter the Kingdom, and if you're rich and great
you're like a heavy-loaded beast stuck in a narrow gate.'

Then Peter says to Jesus, 'You frighten me to death –
I've left my home and everything, and I have nothing left.

It's hard to enter the Kingdom, you know that I have tried,
but at the end, when you go through, will I be left outside?'

'Oh, Peter, Peter,' Jesus said, 'what will I do with you?
I told you: God will get you there if he has to drag you through.'

Roddy Cowie

THE VINE

I am a branch
twining from your stem
with leaves catching the sun.

You are the vine,
connecting us to the roots
spread far throughout the ground.

Roots of the Maker,
ground of our being,
source of life-giving love.

Why then should I fear
pruning from your knife?
Space made for fruitful growth.

Cut swiftly,
cut cleanly, Lord Jesus,
but touch gently the
wounded endings.

Chris Polhill

THE KINGDOM OF HEAVEN

The Kingdom of heaven slips between the cracks
in the meaning of words.
The languages of this world cannot contain it.

In the depths of the ocean of our desperation it lies,
a pearl of enormous wealth.
It fills the cavern of our need.

It soothes the pain that fills the corners of a prison cell.
It pours into the cup of suffering passed around in an upstairs room.

It is the immensity of small acts of compassion.
It is the sea of living water
contained in a single tear of our contrition.

It is the split second between the welling up of joy
and the eruption of laughter.
It is dancing to our own beat.

It is the wide eyes of a child.
It is the filling of our lamps with expectation
for the bridegroom at the end of time.

It is the seed for our hope of life.
It is here.
It is now.

Alizon Sharun

STORYTELLER

O storyteller,
you sit me down
and fill me with tears
and love
and laughter.

Come into my life,
and tell your story
through me.

Ruth Burgess

WATER OF LIFE

O, I will give
the springs of the water of life
to all who thirst;
I will make all things new;
and all who stand firm
will know my blessing.
For I will be your God,
I will be your God.

da Noust

ON HIS WAY

(Luke 4:16–30)

A: It began all right.

B: Nothing out of the ordinary then?

A: Oh no – it's always nice to see one of our own young people helping with the service.

B: He did a reading?

A: That's right. A lovely clear voice. I could hear every word in the back pew.

B: Were there many there?

A: All the usual folk. His family of course.

B: His mother must have been proud.

A: Well yes, but then ...

B: Was it something he said?

A: He was reading from Isaiah. We'd heard it before. I mean, it's traditional. But he made it sound different.

B: 'The Spirit of the Lord'?

A: 'The Spirit of the Lord'.

B: Some people go on a bit about the Spirit. And waving their arms. I am sure they're sincere, but I can't be doing it at my age.

A: What worried me more was 'He has chosen me to bring good news to the poor.'

B: Chosen you?

A: No, that's what the prophet said, and that's what he read, but as though he meant it ... and what does it mean anyway by 'the poor'?

B: Well, we're none of us well-off. We all have to pay these terrible taxes. And keep up appearances.

A: Quite – and 'poor' are them out there. The ones who don't pay taxes.

B: Don't care about appearances.

A: Scroungers.

B: Too many children!

A: Well, what's good news to them? Us having to cough up a bit more!

B: Of course there are widows and orphans and strangers at the gate. Tragic, really.

A: Charity – that's different. It's heart-warming to give to a cause.

B: It's more blessed to give than to receive.

A: And our people are ever so good at giving.

B: Though it's one appeal after another.

A: But what's 'good news' to the poor, for goodness sake? And what's it got to do with us? We are doing our best. Surely we are not expected to change.

B: Did he go on?

A: Go on? It got worse. I couldn't believe my ears: 'He has sent me to proclaim liberty to the captives.'

B: That's what it says in Isaiah.

A: But I always thought it was about the Messiah, some time in the future, a good way off. When he read it I suddenly thought: 'What if it happened now?'

B: There's a lot of folk that are better off behind bars. There's no smoke without fire.

A: Quite. And I can't see the authorities taking kindly to this liberation talk.

B: I just don't see the need.

A: 'And recovery of sight to the blind.'

B: Eh?

A: What does it mean?

B: You never asked that before!

A: 'To set free the oppressed.' Who's oppressed? Them out there? But that's part of the system. You've got to have some on top to give orders, and some underneath to carry them out.

B: That's the way the world keeps going.

A: But who are we? Are we the oppressors or the oppressed?

B: No one's calling me an oppressor – I'll soon settle them ... But why are you worrying? This is only an old prophecy. It's about then and there, not here and now.

A: Unless 'The time has come when the Lord will save his people.'

B: Come on now!

A: But that's what he said, when he finished reading and sat down. He said: 'This passage of scripture has come true today, as you heard it being read.'

B: I don't get it.

A: Nor did we. First we were impressed. After all we'd known him since he was so high. But he was right when he said we'd find it hard to understand him. All we wanted to do was to hear comforting words about God at work far away.

B: I know. Nothing political. Nothing that makes you feel got at or guilty – though you might take up a special offering for some project.

A: But he was bringing it all home. And then having the cheek to tell us that we are only on the edge of what God is doing.

B: You must have been mad.

A: We'd had enough. We showed him just what we thought of his 'good news'. We have a way of dealing with folk who dare to say we are in God's way.

B: And Jesus …

A: He went on his way!
He went on his way …

Jan Sutch Pickard

THE COMMANDMENTS

For some folk, the Ten Commandments *have* to be followed without question. They are the core of how folk are to live; they are the Law; they are the instruments by which we determine who are the really good people, and who are the rotten scoundrels.

For others, the Commandments are a sort of moral code that, while not absolute, gives us some guidance on how we should live.

Yet, for Jesus, keeping the Commandments was an act of love! (John 14:15). Not an act of unquestioning obedience; not a philosophical pondering of the relevance of the Commandments for ourselves and our times; no, simply the natural result of a life lived with God.

If we live life in love with God, how can we not want to keep the Commandments?

Thom M Shuman

SETTING A HAND TO THE PLOUGH
(Luke 9:57–62)

This act of commitment was first offered in Iona Abbey.

In many rural communities there are available on farms horse-drawn, hand-held ploughs of the kind that were used in traditional agriculture before the advent of the tractor. It was to such a plough as this that Jesus referred in his warning to would-be followers to set their hand to the plough and not look back. It was just such a plough that was brought into the Abbey and placed before the communion table, and to which participants in the worship were invited to set their hands.

Introduction

Leader: In many farming communities there is each year a ploughing match to see who can drive the straightest furrow. It is very instructive to watch what the ploughmen and women actually do.

In one category of ploughing with a tractor, they very slowly drive a straight furrow, sometimes with a helper behind to adjust the ploughshare to ensure that it is well-aligned. The ploughman at the wheel of the tractor looks forward and back, forward and back to ensure that he is driving the furrow in a perfect line in parallel with the previous furrow.

The competition is judged. The winner is announced at the end – and sometimes the only person who agrees with the decision of the judges is the ploughman or woman who has come first!

In Palestine, in the days of Jesus, a ploughman could not look back. In many places there were, as there still are, outcrops of rock in the fields and the ploughman had to keep looking ahead to guide the oxen to ensure that the ploughshare did not hit a rock. If he didn't do this, he might very well break his share, and any further ploughing with that share would be impossible.

Reading: Luke 9:57–62

(This may be offered in dramatised form.)
The scene: a crowded street in Israel
The characters: The Evangelist, Jesus, first man, second man, third man, a crowd

The Evangelist: As they went on their way, a man said to Jesus:

First man: I will follow you wherever you go.

Jesus: Foxes have lairs and birds have nests, but the Son of Man has nowhere to lie down and rest.

The first man leaves slowly, with his head down.
A second man runs up to Jesus.

Jesus: Follow me.

Second man: Lord, first let me go back and bury my father.

Jesus: Let the dead bury their own dead. You go and proclaim the Kingdom of God.

The second man draws back into the crowd.
A third man runs up to Jesus.

Third man: I will follow you, sir, but first let me go and say goodbye to my family.

Jesus: Anyone who starts to plough and then keeps looking back is of no use to the Kingdom of God.

The third man departs quickly.

Jesus: (turning to the crowd) Anyone who starts to plough and then keeps looking back is of no use to the Kingdom of God.

Reflection

Those who heard Jesus speaking knew exactly what he meant when he said, 'Anyone who starts to plough and then keeps looking back is of no use to the Kingdom of God.'

The three men who offered to follow Jesus were restrained from following by looking backwards

  – back to a secure life without hardship or risk
  – back to family obligations and responsibilities

So, when we offer to make a commitment to follow Jesus, we are committing ourselves to a future with him, which may well involve risk and hardship and a new set of ties and relationships.

Act of commitment

Leader: At the front of the church, at the communion table, there is a hand-held plough of a type that would have been used in earlier days in this country, and which is similar to the kind used in the time of Jesus.

As an act of commitment I will go forward and simply touch the handles of the plough. In a moment of silence, I will offer myself once more for the service of Jesus, before returning to my seat. You are invited to do the same, if you feel that it is right for you to do so. Some may prefer to remain in their seats and make their own personal commitment there.

Prayer

Of those who would follow Jesus, O God, you demand a decisive commitment. Help us to discern the task to which you call us and the cost of discipleship. Give us, we pray, the assurance that we do not go forward alone but in your company, and in the company of fellow servants of your Kingdom. Give us the strength, we pray, to put our hands to the plough, to hold our course and to fulfil our task in the service of your Kingdom through Jesus Christ, our Lord. Amen

Graeme Brown

PEOPLE JESUS HEALED

MORE THAN I'D EVER BARGAINED FOR

(John 4:5–30)

Read John 4:5–30

Some questions (alone or with others)

Imagine you are at the well:
How might Jesus see you?
What would Jesus say to you?
What would you want to say to Jesus?
How might Jesus change you, refresh you, renew you ...?

Prayer

Jesus,
you meet us at the well.
You teach us that
we are loveable children of God,
and that it is love
which makes everything possible.

You refresh us.
You are our life force,
our vitality,
our energy.

May we share your gifts of love and life
with everyone we meet. Amen

Rosie G Morton

PRAYERS BASED ON JOHN 6

Lord Jesus, you fed the 5,000 with plenty to spare.

We pray for those who are starving,
especially for those in the famine-stricken areas of ...
Lord, feed them:
FEED THEM WITH YOUR BREAD.

Lord, you had faith to walk on the water.
We pray for those who face tasks and difficulties just as daunting.
Lord, feed them:
FEED THEM WITH YOUR BREAD.

Lord, you taught the crowds and extended their understanding.
We pray for those who are hungry for your truth,
reaching out to extend their knowledge and love of you.
Lord, feed them:
FEED THEM WITH YOUR BREAD.

Lord, you shared with us your body and blood.
We pray for those who are eating the bread of affliction
and drinking the cup of suffering.
In their distress feed them;
comfort them with the life which comes from you.
Lord, feed them:
FEED THEM WITH YOUR BREAD.

Lord, you taught us that by eating your flesh and drinking your blood,
we would find eternal life.
We pray for all at the end of their lives.
We pray that they might find their rest in your eternity.
Lord, feed them:
FEED THEM WITH YOUR BREAD.

Anne Lawson

O JESUS HE SPAK NOT A WORD

O Jesus he spak not a word,
he'd not one word to say,
and still they circled him and her
like vultures round a prey:

'She's taken in the very act
fair reekin' frae the bed.
Moses said we should stane her deid
but what say you?' they said.

But Jesus answered not a word,
he'd not one word to say:
his finger traced upon the dust
what winds would blow away.

'Come on and gie's your judgement, sir,'
they chid him to reply;
he took his staun' and measured them,
a glint was in his eye.

'Wha's clean among you let him first
cast at her stanes,' he said,
then stooped again, and, in the dust,
wrote what no man has read.

O Jesus answered that one word,
he'd no more word to say;
but when he lifted up his head
they'd melted all away.

'Whaur's your accusers now?' he asked,
she stood before him lane.
'Wha has seen fit to sentence you?'
She whispered, 'Nane, Lord, nane.'

'Then I don't damn you either, lass,
go from their evil snare
free as a lintie on the wing –
and mind you sin nae mair.'

O Jesus spak but that one word,
he'd no more word to say,
but what he said by what he did
has power till Judgement Day.

Words and music: Ian M Fraser
Arrangement: Donald Rennie

MORE THAN ENOUGH

(Matthew 14:13–21)

There was more than enough grief for Jesus:
he had just got the news that his beloved cousin John
had been beheaded by Herod.

There were more than enough people:
5,000 gathered to hear Jesus – probably
closer to 15-20,000, counting women and kids.

There was more than enough need:
the people were hungry;
they had been with Jesus all day.

There was more than enough fear:
'Jesus, make them go away –
we barely have enough for ourselves.'

But what they did have
was more than enough for Jesus:
who took, who blessed, who broke, who shared
the simple gifts the disciples had –
and it was more than enough for everyone.

When we wonder *Is it enough?* –
what we do for the needy;
what we do about the violence in our world;
what we do about reaching out to young people;
what we do with our simple gifts –

we should remember this story
and think of the promise
that Jesus does not call us to serve in ways
he is unable to equip us.

For he takes, he blesses, he breaks, he shares
our simple gifts with others,
and that will always be
more than enough.

Thom M Shuman

WHISPERS

It was only
whispers
at first,
people averting their eyes,
gossip trickling out
the sides of their mouths
about her 'problem':
the years filled with
laughter, ridicule, rebuke.

Telling stories to his friends,
trading jokes with lawyers,
asking riddles of preachers:
she heard the
whisper
of his robe's hem
as it brushed
the streets of the kingdom.

If I could only touch it, she
whispered,
and did.

In the silence,
no one heard the
whispers
of grace
flowing through her soul,
making her whole.

In the silence,
Jesus tenderly lifted her
to her feet:
'You are well,
daughter of faith,
go in peace'
was the benediction
he
whispered.

Thom M Shuman

THE TWO WOMEN
(Mark 5:21–43)

(Tune: Gaelic lullaby)

Jairus, an important man,
had a daughter very ill,
he to Jesus quickly ran,
begging, 'Heal her if you will!
Come home and touch her,
touch her, touch her.
Come home and touch her,
so that she'll be well again.'

They hurried off without delay,
there wasn't any time to waste.
A crowd of people in their way
slowed them down and cooled their haste.
'Hurry to touch her,
touch her, touch her.
Hurry to touch her,
so that she'll be well again.'

There was a woman in the crowd,
she'd been ill for twelve long years;
tired and lonely with head bowed,
she said through her tears and fears,
'I'll reach and touch him,
touch him, touch him.
I'll reach and touch him,
so that I'll be well again.'

Secretly she bent down low,
gently touched his garment's hem,
felt a strange and warming glow
and knew that she was well again.
She reached and touched him,
touched him, touched him.
She reached and touched him
and knew that she was well again.

Jesus felt her needy hand
even in that busy crowd;
he called her out to come and stand
and this to her he said aloud,
'Daughter, you touched me,
touched me, touched me.
I'm glad you touched me,
your faith has made you well again.'

'But Jairus' daughter, she is dead,'
the mourners wail with might and main.
Jesus, calmly, to them said,
'I'm going to wake her up again!
I'll reach and touch her,
touch her, touch her.
I'll reach and touch her
and I will make her well again.'

He came and took her by the hand,
'Get up, my dear,' he gently said,
'come out of bed, beside me stand,
we'll get your dinner table laid.'
He reached and touched her,
touched her, touched her.
He reached and touched her
and she was made quite well again.

Jesus, come and bless and heal
each son and daughter here today
as faithfully we come to kneel
before you and together pray.
Reach out and touch me,
touch me, touch me.
Reach out and touch me,
in loving make me whole again.

Leith Fisher

ANOTHER WORKING DAY

Just another working day; you could call it ordinary time. I sit gazing at the computer hoping for wisdom. The phone may ring; someone may drop in. I'll head out to the workshop shortly to see how things are coming along.

I've been wondering what was an ordinary working day for Jesus and the disciples. Did healing the sick and teaching the good news ever get tedious for them? What did it take to make a memorable day that they'd talk about over a cup of wine in the evening?

I wonder if they talked about the woman who touched Jesus's cloak:

> *… a large crowd pressed around him. Among them was a woman who had been suffering from haemorrhages for twelve years. She had suffered a lot from her doctors too, and had spent all her money on them. Far from being healed, she got worse. She had heard about Jesus, and edged up behind him in the crowd. She touched his cloak, because, as she said to herself, 'If I only touch his clothes, I will be well again.' Immediately, her haemorrhage stopped; and she knew that she was healed.*
>
> *Knowing that power had left him, Jesus turned and said, 'Who touched my clothes?' 'See this crowd jostling you?' said one of the disciples. 'How can you say, "Who touched me?"' But he looked around to see who had done it, and the woman, knowing what had happened to her, came to him shaking with fear. She fell to her knees, and told him the truth. He said to her, 'Daughter, your faith has made you well; go in peace, and be healed.' (Mark 5:24–34)*

It's a story that stands out for me, and it's among my favourites from the Bible. It's not the healing that stays with me; it's the confident faith of an ordinary person who would rather have been unseen and unknown; someone who took her faith for granted. The faith was alive within her: a certainty that her closeness to Jesus would draw on God's Spirit and heal her body.

I think that the woman knew that the Holy Spirit, Jesus and God were one, and she knew that they were close, close enough to touch, and they still are.

Too many prayers for intercession include the conditional 'If it be your will', or words to that effect. If we need to use those words to protect us from disappointment, then that unknown, quiet woman is far ahead of many of us in her faith.

O my God
nobody knows better than you how frail are this mind and body
Give me the wisdom to tell the difference between my will and yours
Give me the strength to carry the burdens of mind and body
that this life brings
Give me the wit to look down to avoid the pitfalls
and at the same time the will to look up at the glories of creation

Let me see beyond today's cares
Let me celebrate and sing
Let me never forget that all prayers are answered
Let me know that I am part of that glory of creation
and let others see you in me
These things I pray
like the woman who had faith

Andrew Foster

AT THE WEDDING OF JAIRUS'S DAUGHTER
(Mark 5:21–43; Matthew 9:18–26; Luke 8:40–56)

Pipes and lyres and drums.
Moonlight.
Brightly dressed musicians, tapping their feet in time.
Dancers whirling, clapping, laughing.
And, in the middle – faces flushed, eyes only for each other –
Deborah, the bride, and Jacob, her boyish groom.
A living tableau of joy and vitality.

A big wedding this. No expense spared.
After all, Jairus is President of the synagogue.
Months of preparation; people coming and going;
animals slaughtered; flowers arranged;
wine and beer brewed; breads baked; cheeses matured –
cakes and fruit and honey.

I myself travelled quite a distance to be here.
I couldn't miss it.
She's very special, Deborah, though we rarely meet.

Almost like my own daughter.
I had a daughter once, though no one remembers any more.
Only me – I will never forget her.
Stillborn.
She was perfectly formed and looked so peaceful
as I held her tiny body and tried to breathe warmth into it.
Had she lived, she too would be seventeen and ripe for marriage.
I can handle the sadness now, and think of her without that awful weight of pain.

It's five years since the miracle.
Five years since the pipers played a different tune for Deborah.
I remember the wailing and weeping and mournful chants that herald death,
outside this very house.
The day was hot, the crowds suffocating.
I was far from well.
After I delivered and buried my baby
my life was one of constant pain,
physical and emotional torture.
I bled continually.
Sometimes I could only lie in bed and pray for death.
I had heard about this Jesus and how He cured people,
and some little, submerged hope made me follow the crowds,
hoping to catch a glimpse.
I was there when Jairus begged His help.
I saw His look of sympathy.
The crowd was pushing.
He was so close that, instinctively,
I reached out and touched the fringe of His coat.
It was instantaneous.
A physical feeling of warmth – and the bleeding stopped.
For the first time in twelve years I felt energy coursing through this weary body.
He felt it too.
He asked who had touched Him.
I wanted to slip away.
His friends laughed, protesting about the jostling crowds.
But He insisted and asked again,
'Who touched me?'
I was afraid. I was considered unclean and contaminated those I touched.
I feared His censure but, remembering His regard for Jairus,
I came forward, trembling, whispering, 'It was I, Rabbi.'
His smile and the warmth of His voice dispelled all my fears.
He said my faith had healed me.

It was only the beginning.

A messenger came from Jairus's house to say that Deborah had died.
I will never forget how the colour drained from his face.
Jesus took Jairus's arm and said, 'Let us go to your home.'
On arrival He dismissed the pipers and dirge singers and ordered quiet.
I followed the messenger into the house and watched from the doorway.
Jairus's wife, Sarah, was distraught and my own heart overflowed with sorrow.
The little body lying there brought it all back;
and I remember thinking my daughter too would be twelve years old.
I shall never forget what happened next.
Jesus said, 'Talitha kum.'
My heart opened and all the anguish poured out.
Tears coursed down my cheeks.
'Talitha kum.' 'Wake up, little girl.'
It was what I had been saying, deep in my being, every day for twelve years.

Deborah sat up then and said she was hungry.
I felt this enormous happiness.
Something in me too had wakened with His words,
and I knew for certain that life is more than what we see.
Somehow my little one had heard these words too.
'Talitha kum.'
I had some bread and offered it to Deborah.
She smiled and said: 'I had a lovely dream,' then ate the bread, hungrily.

Since then we've always had a special bond.
One day, last year, I even told her about my baby.
When I heard about the wedding I got busy.
I'm a neat needle-worker and make a modest living embroidering garments
and linens for merchants' wives.
I worked a tablecloth with grapes in purple and vine leaves in red and green.
Deborah thanked me profusely and seemed to really like it.
Then she took one of her bridal flowers –
a lily, white and pure and perfuming the night air –
and said, 'For her, you know.'
It touched me greatly.
She disappeared then into the celebration and dancing.
I am content to sit and watch,
arranging the lily carefully on my dress,
pinning it close to my heart.

Mary Hanrahan

JESUS HEALS A MAN WITH PARALYSIS

(Matthew 9:1–8; Mark 2:1–12)

I look up into my friends' faces
and suddenly
the weight of their expectations
crushes me.

All my life ...
all my life, I've been distorted
by other people's expectations:
parents, wife, children, friends –
all wanting me to be
someone else.

And slowly
over the years
my secret self, my real self,
unknown, unwanted, unloved,
has withered and atrophied
as resentment twisted me.

And now – Jesus;
but I refuse to meet his eye
to make contact
in case he too
has expectations –
sees me as someone
I am not
and never can be.

But I cannot evade his voice
and somehow, from him,
'son' sounds different
carries no oppressive overtones;
only a deep yearning
for someone
known, wanted, loved –

a yearning that unknots
the mockery
my life has become.

And as I stand
and meet his eyes
reflected there is someone I know

as myself.

Pat Bennett

LISTEN TO ME

(Mark 7:31–37)

Listen to me. I want to tell you about something that happened to me a few months ago.

Let me tell you a little of my story first.

I've had a hard life. I was born deaf and with a speech impediment. People used to shout at me, and mime things, to get me to understand them. Because I couldn't really hear them, I didn't know what speech should sound like, so although I could say some words, people still found it hard to understand me.

I got along, I had friends, and they and my family stuck up for me, made sure I was OK. But it was frustrating sometimes, wanting to tell people something and not being able to make them understand me, and having to work so hard to understand what people were trying to tell me.

Then, one day, my friends came to me and told me that there was a stranger in the district and he was a healer. They'd heard that he could make blind people see, lame people walk – and deaf people hear. They wanted me to go with them and find him. They wanted to ask him to heal me.

I wasn't sure. I'd not ever thought about being healed. It had never seemed a possibility.

But they reasoned with me, lots of waving hands and shaking heads, and smiles and beckoning fingers. I decided that it couldn't make things any worse, so what had I to lose by meeting this stranger? They said he was called Jesus.

And so I went with them. It took us a while to find him, this Jesus, he seemed to be always on the move, him and his friends, and all the people who followed him.

My friends told me the stories they were hearing about Jesus. He was a miracle worker, he walked on water, calmed storms, he expelled evil spirits, he had brought a dead child back to life. I was beginning to change my mind about meeting him, but my friends wouldn't let me go home.

Eventually we tracked him down. There were crowds of people all around him. It took a while, but at last my friends and I got near to him, and they spoke to him, and pointed to me, and he turned to face me.

Somehow he managed to take me away from the crowds, and there was just him and me, looking at each other. He had kind eyes. I wanted to trust him.

It was all a bit strange what he did next. He put his fingers into my ears, and then he removed his fingers, spat on them, motioned me to open my mouth, and touched my tongue. And then he looked upwards. I looked up too, and suddenly I could hear – a bird singing! I looked at him and tried to mouth 'Thank you', and found I could hear myself saying it. 'Thank you, Jesus.' I said it clearly. I could hear myself speaking. It was amazing. I cried.

He smiled at me, and then he took me back to my friends. I told them I could hear. They could understand me. Everyone was amazed. He told the crowd not to broadcast what had happened to me, but they did.

Everyone was talking about me, lots of people talked to me, and I talked back. My friends' faces were wide with smiles.

That all happened to me a few months ago.

I still hear about Jesus. They say the authorities are trying to stop him talking and healing. I don't know how they'll manage that.

Thank you for listening to me. I enjoy being able to tell my story. It feels good.

Ruth Burgess

BETHESDA

(John 5:1–15)

(Tune: Gatescarth)

A young witness:

I saw what happened here today,
at the Bethesda pool.
Jesus of Nazareth came this way;
he healed this paralysed man, OK?
Now that was really cool!

A Jewish official:

It's been reported by our man
based at Bethesda pool:
Breaking the Sabbath – that's his plan!
We must stop Jesus if we can!
He must not break the rule!

Formerly paralysed man:

For nearly forty years I sat
by the Bethesda pool.
I couldn't make it – that was that!
But Jesus said: 'Take up your mat.'
At once I was made well.

Whole group:

Let's celebrate this story (Wow!)
of the Bethesda pool.
Think not of rules, or why?, or how?
Believe that Jesus heals us now –
and he will make us whole.

David Lemmon

SYROPHOENICIAN WOMAN

(Mark 7:24–30)

Come in, Rebecca.
Sit down.
Can I get you a drink?
Did you pass Sara on the way in?
It's amazing, isn't it?
You wouldn't believe it's the same girl.
Completely well. No more fits. Full of life and laughter.
Yes, it was Him.
Let me tell you the whole story.
Where to begin?
You know they were here last week?
Well, I was determined to have a word.
I was desperate.
Sara was really bad on Tuesday night.
So come Wednesday morning I went looking for His group.
The hardest part was getting near enough.
You know what these Jews are like.
Think they're God's chosen
and the rest of us are little better than camel dung.
I kept my distance till I figured out who He was.
I don't know what I was expecting
but He was rather small and ordinary-looking.
And tired.
He looked worn out.
My heart fell.
I remember thinking it was useless.
Then I pictured Sara writhing in pain
and before I knew it,
I was there, kneeling at His feet, begging.
'Rabbi, my child is in torment. Please help her.'
His answer left me reeling.
'Must the food meant for the children be given to the dogs?'
His friends loved that.
I could see them exchanging superior glances
and sniggering like children tormenting a bird caught in a trap.
He turned to go.
That was it.
I was dismissed.

Well, you know me, Rebecca.
Can't keep my mouth shut.
I thought, *In for a denarius, in for a shekel,*
and I ran after Him, shouting,
'Rabbi, even the dogs get to eat the crumbs that fall from the table.'
He turned round, exasperated;
couldn't believe my cheek.
Then, suddenly,
He smiled.
It transformed His whole face
and I understood why people gave up everything to follow Him.
He gave me a long look, touched my hand and said:
'Your child is well. Shalom, sister.'
At that moment I knew Sara was cured.
It's hard to explain but there was truth in His voice.
Authority.
His friends looked stunned at the familiar greeting,
and silently cleared a space for me to leave.
I walked slowly and held my head high.
My heart was praising God.

The funny thing is, Rebecca, when I looked into His eyes,
there was compassion there, yes, and kindness.
But something else, too.
I could swear it was gratitude.
It was as if I had given Him something.

Mary Hanrahan

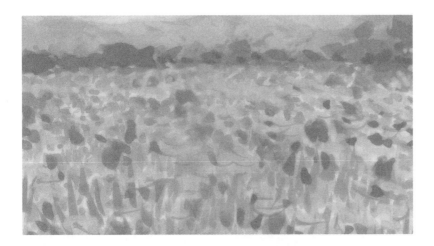

ON THE WAY OF JESUS

THE KINGDOM OF GOD

(This piece was used in Iona Abbey.)

Leader: What is the kingdom of God? I've asked many people what the kingdom of God is for them, and here are some of the answers:

Voice 1:   The presence of Christ in our lives

Voice 2:   Heaven

Voice 3:   All that we receive and know, and all that we don't understand

Voice 4:   Where the rich recognise the poor

Voice 1:   Where we are all one

Voice 2:   Reconciliation

Voice 3:   Within me

Voice 4:   People

Voice 1:   Everyone here

Voice 2:   The rule of God expressed through his people

Voice 3:   Heaven in us

Voice 4:   A fair world for all here on earth

Voice 1:   Our divine potential

Voice 2:   Where we return to when we die

Voice 3:   A place where I can be free and be loved

Voice 4:   Living with Jesus

Voice 1:   Our recognition of Christ's love here on earth

Voice 2:   When really good things happen right here and now and you don't quite know how it happened

Voice 3:   A place where all people and all creation are together in peace, love and harmony and in the complete presence of God

Voice 4:   Living now as if now is heaven ...

Leader: I believe we all have different ideas about what the kingdom of God means to us. And I think that sometimes, if we pay attention, we might be able to see some glimpses of it:

Voice 1: The laughter of a child

Voice 2: Soft warm light on a summer evening

Voice 3: The touch of someone you love

Voice 4: Justice being done

Voice 1: Powerful thunderstorms

Voice 2: A great day at the beach

Voice 3: The breaking down of walls and barriers between families and nations

Voice 4: Brightly-coloured flowers

Voice 1: The smile of a friend

Voice 2: Sitting round a fire

Voice 3: Singing birds

Voice 4: Shared stories ...

Leader: Not only can we see the kingdom – we can make it happen in the world around us, maybe only in little steps, but we can do it. We can do it by caring, by enjoying life, by being fair to each other, by smiling at those around us, by challenging each other, by trying to see each other with the love that God feels for each of us.

We can try to make the little world directly around us a bit lighter, more colourful, more loving and peaceful than it is.

So let's go,
let's do it –
and let's do it now,
without waiting for tomorrow.
As Jesus said: 'Go and announce the kingdom of God!'

Aniko Schuetz

FOLLOW, FOLLOW

Never once, did he say,
'Worship me I am the One.'
Adoration was not sought
or ever needed by the Son.

All he wanted was the heart,
no chant or hollow plea.
The gift he asked? ... 'Release your grasp.
Relax, and follow me.'

Stuart Barrie

GETTING ANGRY

(Mark 1:41)

(In Mark 1:41 Jesus is 'moved with pity'. Other ancient authorities read 'anger' instead of 'pity'.)

I expect Jesus to be compassionate – indeed I count on it. I expect Jesus to feel sorry for people; I expect Jesus to be moved with pity. For pity's sake, this is Jesus we're talking about here! But when he is about to heal someone, I don't expect him to be angry. But he is, in some of the readings that passed among the congregations of the early Church.

He's not angry at being asked to do a healing, but at the misery and injustice that can accompany a physical disability.

He's not angry at the leper, but at the powers that continue to defile God's world, that continue to challenge God's justice – that continue to separate people from the One who has created them in the divine image.

And so it is with passion, not pity, that Jesus heals the leper. It is with that holy righteousness that cannot stand to see another suffer that Jesus brings hope to this outsider. It is with that divine willingness to stand with those who have been cast out by the world – those who have been judged unworthy by society, those who have been condemned because they are not as wealthy or 'wise' or 'wonderful' as we – that Jesus reaches out and touches the man and, in doing so, brings him back into God's family.

We are so easily moved with pity, we can feel sorry for others; we start to complain about compassion fatigue.

Maybe it's time for some passionate anger.

Thom M Shuman

ON THE UPSIDE-DOWN ROAD

(Mark 10:32–45)

(Tune: Ich halte treulich still)

We see you stride ahead,
the dark road stretches on.
With purpose firm, Jesus, you walk
until your work is done.
We often lag behind,
uncomprehending still,
fearful of heart, confused in mind,
irresolute of will.

Disciples argue yet
o'er status, place and power.
Lured on by fashion and esteem,
we miss the vital hour
when, to our startled eyes,
the world turns upside down –
now humble service is the way
of greatness and renown.

We gather, servant Lord,
we see your love made plain.
Give us fresh courage, greater love
to take your way again.
May your abundant grace
give us the grace to be
folk who reflect our Saviour's face
in lives of service free.

Leith Fisher

A RIGHT RELATIONSHIP

This prayer could be read by two voices.

Here's a man,
tramping the dusty roads of his country,
drawing inspiration from the land,
loving its fruitfulness,
sailing its waters,
stilling its storms.

We thank you for our lands and geography,
and for the people,
some of them nomadic as he was,
who are also moved by their love
to struggle for a right relationship between land and people.

Here's a man,
born to a mother who broke the rules and said 'yes',
parented by a man who was not his father,
knowing his ancient lineage
yet calling people to be born again into a new community.

We thank you for our families and history,
and for the people,
some of them single parents,
who bear love back into the world
and struggle for a right relationship between persons.

Here's a man,
throwing up a steady job to follow his calling,
keeping bad company, often sleeping rough,
touching people who were considered untouchable,
raising up those who were overlooked.

We thank you for all who have trusted us, believed in us and valued us,
and for the people, homeless, jobless, unappreciated, some of them,
who will not let their dreams or spirits die,
and who struggle for a right relationship within communities.

Here's a man,
refusing to be less than free,
refusing to be less than utterly committed,
refusing to bow down and serve the empires of the world.

We thank you for all whose faith and courage has kept alive for us
the vision of God's Kingdom,

and for the people, mocked and persecuted some of them,
who struggle for a right relationship among the nations.

Young man Jesus,
in tenderness, justice and joy,
in forgiving and healing,
you lived the promise of a new relationship with God,
you died making it real,
and as the new branches spring from the deepest roots
when the tree is cut down,
your life, grounded in God, could not be destroyed.
In joy and sorrow,
in failure and accomplishment,
bring us into right relationship with the God of love and life.

Kathy Galloway

WE KNOW FINE WELL

What in heaven's name do we mean when we pray every day, 'Thy Kingdom come, thy will be done on earth as it is in heaven'? What does that mean?

We know fine well what the Kingdom values are, in broad precept if not in detail, and they're not about narrow religious issues, they're about the basic stuff of human life. They're the stuff of the Sermon on the Mount.

The Kingdom values are about money and possessions and power and sex and violence and security; about war; about how we treat our neighbour; about how we treat our enemy. Fine well we know God's will and we cannot hide behind ignorance.

We know God's will about flowers blooming in wilderness places, about the blind being able to see, the deaf hearing, the lame leaping and dancing and the dumb shouting aloud. It's about drug addicts and AIDS sufferers and the homeless young in 'cardboard cities' being valued and brought in from the cold.

God's will is about those who are 'rubbished' and dismissed being treasured; it's about the powerful being brought to heel; about the first being last and the last first.

It's good news to the poor; about feeding the hungry and clothing the naked; about liberty to the captives and setting free the oppressed; about the time having come when the Lord will save his people.

These are the Kingdom values; that is the Kingdom agenda and we know it well. We cannot hide behind ignorance. We cannot say we do not know … we know, fine well!

Erik Cramb

MEDITATION ON THE LORD'S PRAYER

Our Father in heaven,
Father, I sense you
in busyness, creativity and frustrations of the workplace,
in laughter and tears of the family home,
in conflict and peace-making in the world,
in the red-bracken mountain climb ...
Open my eyes to glimpses of your heaven
each day.

Hallowed be your name,
You call my name,
you call me to worship –
to sing and dance,
to shout and proclaim,
to give praise to your name.

Your kingdom come,
You call me to be your servant,
to be your love in the world,
to further your kingdom on earth.
Show me, guide me, how to serve you.

Your will be done,
That is my daily prayer.
What is your will for your people?
What is your will for your world?
What is your will for me?
I listen for your voice;
show me the path to follow.

On earth as in heaven.
May I live your will
in the small daily acts of living
and in the way I respond to your call.
May I work your will
here and now on earth,
with a vision of your glory,
the inspiration of your kingdom before me.

Give us this day our daily bread;
You provide for my needs,
my food and shelter;

give me strength to serve you,
wisdom and knowledge
so I may share your gospel,
love and compassion
so I may live and work your good news.

Forgive us our sins as we forgive those who sin against us;
Forgive me for those days and years,
those perplexing times,
when I failed to respond to your call;
for times when I doubt your power to equip me for the task;
for holding back when I should step forward;
for remaining silent when I should speak.
May I forgive those who hurt me,
who doubt me, or overlook me.

Lead us not into temptation,
May I not be tempted to divorce action from prayer,
nor prayer from action.
May I not give way to complacency,
nor undue fear,
to arrogance,
nor timidity.
Grant me patience to test my sense of calling
with humility and the wisdom of others.
May I proceed with deep honesty and integrity.

But deliver us from evil.
Help me to keep to the path
that leads to you,
and to avoid patterns of living that keep me from you.

For yours is the kingdom, the power and the glory,
for ever and ever. Amen
As your servant,
may I partake in the growth of your kingdom;
may I sing and work to your praise and glory.

Father and Mother in heaven,
let your power work in my life.

Amen

Judy Dinnen

GOD'S WILD CARD

Gentle Jesus, meek and mild,
cried the house down as a child.
Swaddling bands applied too tight
gave mum many a sleepless night.

Gentle Jesus, meek and mild,
grew an awkward God-willed child:
in the temple caused a fuss,
taught the teachers, missed the bus.

Gentle Jesus, meek and mild,
when a woman was defiled,
made accusers slink away
self-accused, that judgement day.

Gentle Jesus, meek and mild,
taught: God is not race-beguiled,
counts as equal, as God can,
woman, Jew, Samaritan.

Gentle Jesus, meek and mild,
where the money pots were piled
turned the tables, made a space,
there restored folk's praying place.

Gentle Jesus, meek and mild,
scourged, from angel power resiled;
treated as if human dross
bowed his head, took up his cross.

Gentle Jesus, meek and mild,
trusted women (men were riled)
to announce his risen brief;
killing death, assuaging grief.

Gentle Jesus, on his throne,
will not stomach words alone:
'If your words with deeds don't gel
you're not mine: so go to Hell!'

Ian M Fraser

*Note: Translations of the gospels may do less than
justice to some of the rough talk in them. In a*

carol, we are asked to sing 'the baby awakes, but little Lord Jesus no crying he makes'. ('Some hope!' says Mary in heaven.)

Jesus bawled out the disciples when they kept the children from him (the Greek word aganakteo *is stuffed with over-the-top irritation). He bawled out Peter when he tried to divert him from anticipating the Cross, calling him 'Satan'. Ironing out some rough stuff does a theological disservice. It reduces the reality of the Incarnation. Jesus was as human as they make them.*

STORAGE SPACE

'Don't store up your treasures in barns where thieves can break in and steal them. Store up your treasures in heaven ...'

I want an opt-out clause
for functional, flexible, flat pack storage solutions.

Metre upon metre of my stuff, my self,
forms a barrier
protecting me from you.

Storing props and costumes:
Vicar girl, Adventure girl, Business girl, Party girl.
Without my Barbie-styled identities
I am nothing. No one. A nonentity.
But not to you.

Floods float away false identities, cunning disguises.
Leaving in their wake:
raw nakedness
true self.
Graced,
loved,
treasured in heaven.

Karen Jobson

POOR IN SPIRIT

'Blessed are the poor in spirit,
for theirs is the Kingdom of heaven.'
Right!
You said it, Lord,
so it must be true.
But
I'm not feeling very blessed just now.
So help me please.
My self-confidence is at an all-time low;
my faith, once a beacon
by which others found their way
and warmed themselves,
has shrunk to
a wee guttering candle.

My hope,
'the vision' which once inspired me,
has been clouded over
by my mistakes.
And love?
I just see hurt, painfully clearly
in those I love
and in those who love me.

I am spiritually broke, then!
Utterly skint,
on my uppers.
The good I long to do
I get all wrong.
The mistakes I abhor,
I seem to have made.
I've had it!
So,
like a beggar I cry for mercy.

Is there any hope for me?
After all, Saint Paul found much the same!
So maybe there is.

Ian Cowie

SAINTS

ST JULIAN'S DAY

(8th May)

(Tune: Truro)

All shall be well! Thus down the years
the words to Julian once declared
re-echo like a song of hope
to sing among today's despairs.

All shall be well! The power of sin
shall not, at last, victorious be;
but love that made and makes us whole
shall fill the whole eternity.

All shall be well! Our mother Christ,
who heals our wounds in Christ the Son,
who seals us with the Spirit's love,
shall make the sin-divided one.

All shall be well! These words of God
have greater power than we can tell.
God holds the world. The world responds
in love: 'God loves! All shall be well.'

David Fox

PARAPHRASE OF ALTUS PROSATOR*

(Tune: Blow the candles out, 8686)

The mighty sower, God unborn,
gave all the worlds their frame;
he threw the ancient serpent down
and bound him fast in flame.
He raises clouds from boundless seas
and sifts the shining rain
so rivers water fertile lands
and flow to sea again.

His arm will bring the end of days;
in darkness and in cloud
the first Archangel's trumpet call
will echo clear and loud.
The book of conscience opened wide

makes every action known,
as wakened souls return to flesh
and bone returns to bone.

When Christ, the Most High Lord, returns
above the ruined sky,
too bright for human eye to bear,
the cross will shine on high.
The sun and moon will hide their light,
the stars like fruit will fall;
and armies turn and hide in fear
as fire sweeps over all.

Then high above the roaring sound
the angels' song will rise;
with them the four great creatures sing
and lift their thousand eyes.
The elders stand in robes of white
and raise their burning crowns
and throw them down beneath the Lamb
and join the glorious sound.

For those whose hearts are fixed below
on riches in this earth,
that awful fire ends all they had,
their pleasure and their worth.
But those whose hearts are fixed beyond
the flame will raise on high
to join the host before the Lamb,
to sing, and never die.

Now to God who gave us life,
to Christ, his mighty son;
now to his eternal Spirit
binding us in one;
let angels, saints and mortals
sing glory without end.
As it was when light first shone,
and evermore: Amen

Roddy Cowie

* High or deep sower of seed. Altus Prosator is a long Latin hymn attributed to St Columba.

ST COLUMBA'S DAY

(9th June)

Colum, Irish prince
you caused the slaughter of 3,000
and fled to Iona
to save as many souls.

Columcille, monk
in your beehive cell
you slept on a bed of bracken,
your pillow stone.

Columba, saint
you wrought hope
from despair, light from dark,
let us go and do the same.

Mary Palmer

GREAT GOD OF THE ELEMENTS

A prayer of approach

Great God of the elements,
you call us to beauty and to glory
and we wonder.

Bright Jesus of Galilee,
you call us to joy and to justice
and we say 'Yes'.

Holy, strong and life-giving Spirit,
you call us to be saints
and we squirm.

You know us, God.
You know our hopes and our dreaming.
You know our failures and our fears.

Pardon us, God,
we seek your mercy.
Smile on us,
we seek your face.

(silence)

Listen,
God speaks to us in Jesus:
I love you.
Your sins are forgiven.
Come and follow me.
I am your way home.

Thanks be to God. Amen

Ruth Burgess

SAINTS IN MELTDOWN

'Let's melt down the saints and put them back into circulation.' Oliver Cromwell

In times past
saints were worth their weight in gold.
Their deeds were applauded,
their faith was esteemed,
their deaths honoured.

In our times
sinners luxuriate under the weight of other people's gold.
The deeds of self-centred entrepreneurs are applauded,
the many-faceted faiths of conmen and charlatans are esteemed,
the deaths of unworthy celebrities are honoured.

Now is the time
for meltdown;
saints putting themselves back into circulation:
fool's gold
exchanged for gold from the Refiner's fire.

Pam Hathorn

THE FAIR FLOWER OF WALES

A story for telling

All of this happened, if it happened at all, in the seventh century after Christ's birth …

I suppose it all began with my mother's brother, Uncle Beuno: strong, sure of himself, long-winded sometimes, terrible temper, and in the pulpit, a real Welsh ranter – ablaze, on fire for God. And what a God! Moses, Welsh druid, Obi-Wan Kenobi, Gandalf … all shaken together and rolled into one!

Living with an uncle like that, and with parents who lived in awe of him, is it any wonder that I grew up knowing that God was all around me, and that the idea of giving my life to God, becoming a nun, was planted early into my body and soul?

My uncle encouraged me, grilled me initially, to ensure that my growing friendship with God was no adolescent illusion; then spent time with me, grounding me in the words of the Bible, the ways of the church, the mysteries of prayer and praise.

And so I grew, enjoying the beauty of the hills around me, the love of my parents, the guardianship of my uncle, the friendship of God.

And then, that day, that day when the world changed for me. My parents and my uncle were already in church and I was on my way there, having stayed behind to ensure that the food was cooking safely.

From nowhere, suddenly standing in my path was Prince Caradoc. I could see by the look in his eyes what he wanted. He grabbed my arm and began to drag me towards the bushes, telling me all the while how much he loved me and that he wanted to marry me.

The more I cried out that I had vowed to become a nun – that I *could not* marry him – the harder he tried to kiss me. The more I refused his advances, the angrier he became. He was used to having everything he wanted. I don't think that anyone had ever said no to him before and he didn't like it.

In his anger he drew his sword and threatened to kill me: If he couldn't have me then no one else was going to have me either. I remember screaming in terror and half hearing my uncle tearing up the hill towards us. I tried to pull away but Caradoc was much stronger than me. I glimpsed him raise his sword arm above me, and then begin to bring it down and then … nothing.

They tried to tell me afterwards what had happened, but everyone had a slightly different version, and in time the stories became more fantastic, more unbelievable, and I'm no longer sure how much of it I can really believe or understand.

Apparently Caradoc had cut my head off with one blow of his sword and my head and body had fallen separately to the ground. Caradoc had stood there, seemingly stunned by what he had done; and he was still standing there when my uncle arrived minutes later. And my uncle cursed Caradoc – cursed him with such a strong and powerful curse that the earth opened up under him and swallowed him, and his body was never found. And then my uncle lifted up my body in his arms and prayed – beautiful fervent prayers; and as he placed my body near to my head, the two were joined and I breathed – I lived!

I remember hearing weeping and praying and running water, and opening my eyes to my uncle's smile and my parents' tears – tears of wonder and overflowing joy.

Beside me, close to the path, apparently on the very spot where my once-severed head had fallen, a new spring of fresh Welsh water bubbled with life and flowed away down the hillside.

That day, what a day – a day that changed my life for ever.

I lived on after that, fifteen years I lived on, and I became a nun and eventually an abbess in a small monastery among the Welsh hills, away from the place of my birth. But I never forgot that day, indeed I had always a thin white scar round my neck to remind me.

I died and was buried quietly near my monastery, but my story was not over. Where my spring was, they made a well, which became famous as a place of pilgrimage and healing, venerated by travelling people, thronged by poor people and visited by royalty. They dug up my bones and enshrined them at Shrewsbury. Later they were mostly destroyed, along with my shrine, during the period they call the Reformation. But nothing destroyed my well, and the pilgrims continued to come.

You can celebrate my life and death on two days each year, once on the anniversary of my martyrdom in June and once on the anniversary of my natural death in November. You can kiss the remaining relics of my body, half of my finger bone in Shrewsbury, the other half at my well. You can read about me in poetry and story★. My well is still open to pilgrims; you can bathe in it, and drink its water.

And my name? You choose. I am the Fair Flower of Wales, the Hope of distressed pilgrims, the patron saint of Holywell. I am Gwenfrewi, Saint Winefride of Wales.

Ruth Burgess

★ *'St Winefred's Well' by Gerard Manley Hopkins; A Morbid Taste for Bones: the First Chronicle of Brother Cadfael by Ellis Peters.*

SAINTS WHO HAVE WALKED OUR ROADS

A Northumbrian prayer

We thank God for the saints who have walked our roads:
for Aidan who refused to give up on us
for Hilda who nurtured us
for Cuthbert who led us
for Josephine who spoke up for prostitutes
for miners from Jarrow who marched for justice
for Bede who wrote our history
for Bega who left footprints in the snow.

God who calls us to be saints,
fill us with laughter and courage,
set us on fire with your love and justice.
Walk with us on our roads. Amen

Ruth Burgess

DEAR ABBOT

A class of schoolchildren in Northumbria were learning about Bede, who, they were told, entered the monastery at St Peter's as a child. They enjoyed helping each other write letters of recommendation about themselves to the Abbot of the monastery:

Dear Abbot, This is Tony. He is strong. He will feed the horses. He helps people. He likes music. He is as strong as a lion.

Dear Abbot, This is David. He will try and work hard. He sleeps well at night. He likes to grow things. He is seven years old. His birthday is on June 4th.

Dear Abbot, This is Emma. She is tall. She likes working. She is a very good reader. She is a good writer. She is a good drawer. She is eight. She looks after her brother and sister, and she wants to look after people who are sick.

Dear Abbot, This is Ian. He will try to work. He can colour in well. His friend is Robert.

Dear Abbot, This is Jonathan. He is a good drawer and writer. He tidies up for me. Jonathan is fussy what he eats. He will like to help to do the pictures in the books.

Dear Abbot, This is Terri. She will be good and she will go to work at the pigsty. She will go to bed at seven o'clock. She will do the dishes.

Dear Abbot, This is Mandy. She would do anything for you. She would make the tea and she would do it properly. She would not stop. She would clean up and her birthday is 12th of June and she is seven.

Dear Abbot, This is Gary. He is good. He is a good worker. When you say go to bed he does.

Dear Abbot, This is Mark. He tries to paint properly.

Dear Abbot, This is Lee. He will like to help you work with history. He would go straight to sleep at night. He is a good boy. He likes his friends very much.

Dear Abbot, This is Katie. She is a good girl. She would like to do all the housework. She likes playing and reading books.

Dear Abbot, This is Philip. He is good. He is strong and does lots of exercises. He will work with Tony. He has big muscles.

Dear Abbot, This is Stacey. She would like to work with some horses. Sometimes she gets a stomach ache and a headache when she goes to bed.

Dear Abbot, This is William. Sometimes he is a fighter. He is polite. He is strong. He likes singing and he wants to learn how to read and write.

Dear Abbot, This is Cindy. She is a hard worker. She would guard the Abbey. She can draw well. She drinks lots of milk. She likes to eat egg sandwiches.

Dear Abbot, This is Haley and she will go to bed at seven o'clock because she is seven years old. She is very good at doing things like washing up. She is good at playing games. She goes to sleep and she never snores.

Dear Abbot, This is Jean Marie. She believes in God and Jesus. She can write with both her hands. Her favourite story is about Jesus. She brushes her teeth every day after breakfast.

Dear Abbot, This is Robert. He is a good boy. When you ask him to go to bed he will and when he gets in bed he will go to sleep. He is a good drawer. He would like to drive the horse and cart.

Dear Abbot, This is Victoria. She is good and kind. She is very pretty. She is a hard worker. She is good at cleaning. She is eight.

Dear Abbot, This is Jade. She is a good worker and likes to do messy jobs. She sometimes sneaks in her brother's bed. She likes to play with friends. She likes sweet things.

Dear Abbot, This is Leanne. When she goes to bed she goes fast asleep. She can dress herself.

Class 2R with Ruth Burgess

FATHER'S DAY

FATHER GOD

Father God
You welcome us
WE ARE GLAD TO CALL YOU
OUR FATHER

Father God
You shelter us
WE ARE GLAD TO CALL YOU
OUR FATHER

Father God
You delight in us
WE ARE GLAD TO CALL YOU
OUR FATHER

Ruth Burgess

WARM US AND HEAL US WITH LOVE

God,
some people find it helpful to call you father,
some don't.

Fathers can be good or bad,
by degrees;
they are rarely neutral.

On a day dedicated to fatherhood,
let there be joy and happiness,
let there also be an acknowledgement of pain and sadness.

God, of moments and of memories,
warm us and heal us with love.

Ruth Burgess

INASMUCHING

(Matthew 25:40 AV)

Inasmuching.
There is of course no such word.
But the way my dad lived
made a verb of it.

A practical man, my dad;
his speciality
was looking after maiden ladies
left over from World War One.
Never a car seat unoccupied
if one of them said 'yes' to an outing
in his beloved Yorkshire Dales.

Not a great man, my dad,
nor entirely a happy man.
Always a sense of life's demands
being heavy for him.
But he shared what he had
and he called it inasmuching.

Josie Smith

OUR FATHER

Our Father
who art also our Mother,
our Brother,
our Sister,
our Lover,
our Friend.

Thank you for being who you are
and who you will be,
world without end.
Amen

Ruth Burgess

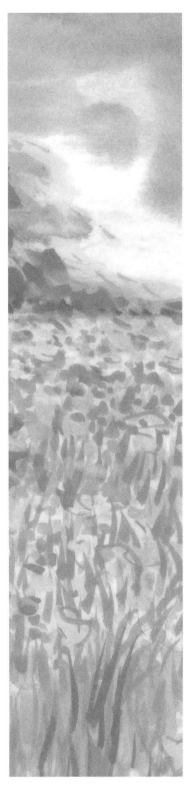

MAN

I can
kick the shit
out of you
if you want me to
I can
drink like a fish
roar like a bull
be full
of myself.
I can
conquer, compete,
coerce, defeat.
I can
dominate you
if you want me to.

A man's man
in a man's world
a single
Y chromosome
and a lifetime's conditioning
defining my being.

But
that's not my way
it wasn't my father's
and it won't be my son's.

I walk
alongside
I cry
at beauty
I nurture
my children
I value
my art.

I can
match you
for macho
but

that's not my way.

I'm sorry
if my way
threatens
you.

Pete Anderson

A FATHER'S DAY WISH FOR
AN (ALMOST) ABSENT FATHER

Happy Father's Day!

I'll give you a card and gift today,
a token of my love and affection –
the love and affection I'd long to share
if only you were here more for me.

The choice was never mine
to see so little of you.
So much I've wanted to say to you,
so many things I wanted to do.

I make excuses for you.
You're working long hours away from home.
You have a new partner and family.
You just don't have the time to spend with me.

But I want to know
how much you love me,
whether it's enough
to take time out for me.

I wish the hours spent together today
might be a foretaste of long hours to come;
I long that deep down in your heart
there might be a special place for me.

Judith Jessop

WE GIVE THANKS FOR FAITHFUL MEN

Jesus, son of God,
our brother,
our leader,
we give thanks for faithful men:

for those who followed their heart or their gut
and walked and worked with you those three years of ministry;

for those who, by their action, their thinking or their beliefs,
have made an impact on our lives;

and for those fathers, grandfathers and father figures
who have taught and tended us with a true fatherly love.

We give you thanks for these faithful men.

Jesus, your values are not the world's values.
You teach and show us that
    the weak help the strong,
    the poor lead the rich,
    the foolish teach the wise.

We remember that, by the world's standards, this is absurd,
and that, as Christians,
we see through a different lens,
we measure with a different scale.

And so, in our world of conventions and expectations,

we pray for those men who try hard to be tough
because they're afraid to be tender;

for those courting professional success
while those they love are relative strangers;

for those stifled by the pressure
of living up to who they are supposed to be;

and we pray for ourselves, male and female,
when we have become lured by the world's values,
or have felt forced to conform to them.

Jesus Christ,
Word become human,

barrier-breaker,
healer, teacher, challenger,
role model,
teach us to discover and value the true gifts of our gender,
male and female. Amen

Alison Adam

THE EMBRACE OF GOD'S LOVE

Lord, as I have seen a father lift a crying child,
lift me
into the embrace of your love.

Lord, as I have seen a father lift a hurting child,
lift me
into the embrace of your healing.

Lord, as I have seen a father lift an angry child,
lift me
into the embrace of your calming.

Lord, as I have seen a father lift a frustrated child,
lift me
into the embrace of your liberation.

Lord, as I have seen a father lift a tired child,
lift me
into the embrace of your renewal.

Lord, as I have seen a father lift a helpless child,
lift me
into the embrace of your empowering.

Lord, as I have seen a father lift a happy child,
lift me
into the warm embrace of your love.

Pat Bennett

HYMN FOR FATHER'S DAY

(Tune: Bunessan)

Child in the manger,
friend of the stranger,
mothered by Mary,
conceived by God.
Part of a family,
loving and holy,
how we adore you,
Jesus, our Lord.

Suckled by Mary,
nurtured by Joseph,
learning his trade with
hammer and wood.
Taught by his father
to make yokes easy,
as a good joiner
certainly should.

Today we thank you
for our own fathers,
who with our mothers
teach us your ways;
loving and guiding,
always providing,
hoping and praying,
singing your praise.

Thus may we honour
father and mother,
those you have given
for us to love.
May they be treasured,
gratefully cared for
while our life's measured
by God above.

Murdoch MacKenzie

*'Child in the manger' is the first line of a hymn by Mary
Macdonald, translated by Lachlan Macbean.*

LET US PRAY FOR FATHERS

Let us pray for fathers:
for loving fathers,
for caring fathers,
for absent fathers,
for young fathers,
for cruel fathers,
for brave fathers,
for fathers who have died.
God, who Jesus called father,
HEAR OUR PRAYERS.

Let us pray for fathers who read to their children,
for fathers who have had to watch a child die,
for fathers who provide for their families,
for fathers unable to find work.
God, who Jesus called father,
HEAR OUR PRAYERS.

Let us pray for fathers who have two or more families,
for fathers whose children are adults,
for fathers who have long been in love with their wives,
for fathers who became fathers today.
God, who Jesus called father,
HEAR OUR PRAYERS.

Let us pray,
for our own fathers,
our friends' fathers,
for men unable to father children,
for fathers we know who need our support and our prayers.
God, who Jesus called father,
HEAR OUR PRAYERS.

LOVING GOD,
AS FATHERS,
AS MOTHERS,
AS CHILDREN,
WE ASK FOR YOUR BLESSING
AS WE BRING YOU OUR PRAYERS. AMEN

Ruth Burgess

FATHERS

They didn't have the opportunities we had,
but made more of them.
Without degrees they made their mark
locally, writing in parish magazines.
Proved by the thirties and the War
they knew unemployment
without joyriding.
They knew rationing without resentment.

Our fathers lived life fully
and they lived in us,
our school reports, our foreign holidays,
our student days,
unlikely choice of jobs
and odd liaisons.

Now they are gone, their passing tolled
by every nerve and cell
in us, their grieving sons and daughters.

Eleanor Nesbitt

A BLESSING

May God our father bless us
MAY WE BE STRONG AND BRAVE AND TENDER

May God our mother bless us
MAY WE BE CARING AND ADVENTUROUS AND LOVING

May God our friend bless us
MAY WE SHARE WONDER, SADNESS AND LAUGHTER

May God our lover bless us
MAY WE LIVE TOGETHER IN JUSTICE AND IN JOY. AMEN

Ruth Burgess

SUMMER

THANK YOU

God of golden fields
and blue skies
THANK YOU FOR SUMMER

God of white waves
and wet pebbles
THANK YOU FOR SUMMER

God of ripe plums
and meadowsweet
THANK YOU FOR SUMMER

Thank you for warmth
and beauty and wonder
THANK YOU FOR LIFE

Ruth Burgess

ON THE APPROACH OF MY
SUMMER HOLIDAY

Summer is a time for sleep:

not the sleep of hibernation,
hiding away from the world,
but the sleep of refreshment.

Long relaxing sleep:

that puts the past to rest,
that restores the mind and soul,
that heals the tired body,
that nurtures the future.

Salvation through sleep!

Judith Jessop

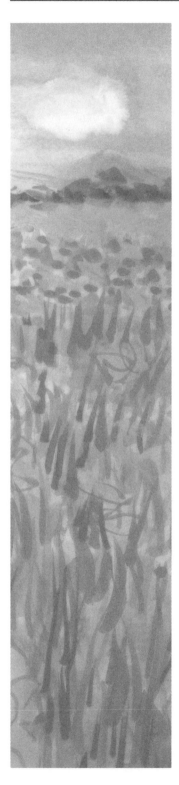

TO GO ON HOLIDAY

People go to work
to get some money
to go on holiday
to have fun
to go to the seaside
to get shells.

Paul, aged 8

SUMMER

Summer suns are glowing
over land and sea;
but they're seldom shining
when they need to be
glowing for my pleasure
on a special day;
summer suns once glowing
now have gone away.

Barbecues and weddings,
summer fêtes and all,
need some sunny weather,
not a stormy squall!
But instead of sunshine
in June or July,
I'm still stuck with storm clouds
darkening the sky.

Summer suns are glowing –
everywhere but here!
Please, God, make it brighter
than it was last year.
And when summer's radiance
warms my days again,
I'll give you the credit –
honest, Lord! Amen

Tom Gordon

DANDELIONS

Bright yellow in the morning light.
Dandelions.
A field chock-full of them.
Beautiful.
What a year for dandelions!

A flower that opens wholly,
holds nothing back.
Exposed and vulnerable,
it offers all it's got;
a sign of life fully lived,
a pathway to the kingdom.

Dandelions.
Beautiful in the sunlight.
Smiling back at their Creator.

Paul Heppleston

PRAYER OF THANKS FOR SUMMER FRUIT

(If possible, pass around a basket of fruit while reading this prayer.)

We thank You, God, for blossom:
its beauty reflects the harvest yet to come.

We thank You, God, for strawberries:
their fullness reminds us of Your grace.

We thank You, God, for raspberries:
they are worth the toil to protect them from the birds.

We thank You, God, for bilberries:
so small and delicate, yet in clumps so rich.

We thank You, God, for apples:
so familiar and reliable, like Your care for us.

We thank You, God, for blackberries:
not fruit from our labour – but we collect them anyway.

Thank You, God, for Your abundant love.

Elizabeth Kime

THE LAKE

The lake was still, tranquil in the morning light.
I, too, was still, watching and listening.
What would God say to me today?

A dragonfly danced and darted,
then rested beside me,
amber-iridescent in the sun.
Being not doing.

God said I could be like that,
being not doing,
receiving his love.

Hilary Allen

THE SHED

I spent a summer once in a shed, in a potato patch.
Quite handy for midnight chips,
and deep and happy sleeps.

Tickled awake by brightening light each day,
lulled to sleep by haunting bird-cry.

The door flung open letting air flood in.
Smells of summer wrapped in salt and seaweed.

The door tightly closed, thunder in the rain,
deafening downpour, and little me snug and dry.

That summer in that shed,
the outer and inner came together,
and peace wrapped me softly.
Warm blanket,
with me cosy inside.

Rachel Shepton

ALL THE HOLIDAYS

Dear God,
Thank you for all the holidays off school.

Christopher, aged 7

SUMMER INTERCESSIONS

City life

Life-giving, life-loving God:
from the sobbing of the rain to the laughter of daisies
your glory is everywhere heard and seen.
The blackbird sings it and the rose is scented with it;
all around us the earth pulsates with it –
your glory, the heartbeat of the universe.

Life-giving, life-loving God,
whose energy and zest for creative action are reflected in our city life:
in business and in study; in science, music and theatre;
in worship and in play.
All around us people are living and dreaming and hoping and working,
showing the divine image in their passion and sense of purpose.

Life-giving, life-loving God,
we offer to you the images we have seen of a world
peopled by a human race which falls far short of its potential:
the scorched earth of Darfur,
where the burnt villages,
the barren fields and the two million displaced people
show our capacity for violence and destruction;
the wasted flesh and visible bones of the children
who are dying from lack of food and preventable diseases,
because we have set our own comforts
higher than our neighbours' basic needs;
the blue-white skin of the teenager addicted to drugs,
who sleeps rough on the streets of the city,
pricking our conscience even as we cross the street to avoid her.

Life-giving, life-saving God,
we offer you, too, the images which help to sustain our hope
in the redemptive power of Jesus Christ:

the chain of coffee carts in UK railway stations which,
due to customer demand, now sells only fairly traded coffee;
the volunteers at Starter Packs in Dundee
who give their time and resources to support homeless people
in making a fresh start in a place of their own;
the people from all walks of life
who are working to keep Africa in the news
and in the minds of the leaders of the G8.

Giver, lover, saviour of life:
strengthen us to play our part
in the story of creation as it continues to unfold.
Help us to give of ourselves and, in doing so, to discover our gifts;
help us to bring life to others and to find a reason to dance for joy.
Amen

Cally Booker

SUMMER SOLSTICE

June 31

Then God said, 'Let there be light', and there was light. And God saw the light, that it was good.' (Gen 1:3–4)

On this day, in Britain, we experience more hours of light from the sun than on any other day. The short, cold days of December seem far away, as we enjoy the long, warm days. In other countries, it is winter, but the light will come round to them too.

'Lord, lift up the light of your countenance upon us.' (Ps 4:6)

Light brings warmth and comfort.
Light shines into dark corners
and shows us that there are no hidden monsters waiting to pounce.
Light reveals the beautiful colours of our world.
Light always shines, even through storms.

'Truly the light is sweet, and it is pleasant for the eyes to behold the sun.' (Eccl 11:7)

Elizabeth Kime

A PRAYER FOR MIDSUMMER

We give thanks for the joy of creation:
for all that is made and given;
for all that we shape and create;
for the springing forth of new vision.
WE CELEBRATE THE FLOWERING OF HOPE.
WE GIVE THANKS FOR THE FRUITS OF THE EARTH.
WE PRAISE THE GODDESS OF GROWTH.

We give thanks for the vitality of re-creation:
for times of rest and stillness that renew us;
for times of play and laughter that refresh us;
for all that nourishes and restores our spirits.
WE CELEBRATE THE FLOWERING OF HOPE.
WE GIVE THANKS FOR THE FRUITS OF THE EARTH.
WE PRAISE THE GODDESS OF GROWTH.

We give thanks for the depth of passion:
for the vision that inspires our longing;
for love that brings strength and tenderness;
for all that touches our deepest core.
WE CELEBRATE THE FLOWERING OF HOPE.
WE GIVE THANKS FOR THE FRUITS OF THE EARTH.
WE PRAISE THE GODDESS OF GROWTH.

We give thanks for the rhythm of the seasons:
for all that grows, blossoms and fades;
for the seeds that are buried and spring again;
for the constant renewal of life from the earth.
WE CELEBRATE THE FLOWERING OF HOPE.
WE GIVE THANKS FOR THE FRUITS OF THE EARTH.
WE PRAISE THE GODDESS OF GROWTH.

Jan Berry

Note: If you prefer, the last line of the response could be:
WE PRAISE GOD FOR THE GOODNESS OF GROWTH.

WEE BEASTS

HAIKUS WRITTEN AT OUR CABIN

Sounds of woodpeckers
hammering distant oak trees,
cut the morning mists.

Dragonflies on wing
clasp the thorax of their mates.
White pond lilies bloom.

Midst quiet aspen,
dusk descends to God's good earth.
Toads trill joyful songs.

Ed Daub

NOT AFRAID

Dear God,
Please would you make my sister
not afraid of spiders?

Jean Marie, aged 7

DEALING WITH HORNETS

Last summer hornets regularly visited us,
three or four times a week.
On warm summer evenings they would fly in
through open windows,
into the kitchen or living room.
There would be one or two,
sometimes three –
once we had an invasion of six.
And they would blunder ponderously round the room
regularly thumping into walls and cupboard doors.
(Don't hornets get headaches?)
I heard a wicked little voice in my head say:
'Hunt them, swat them,
squash them, slay them.
Keep a daily tally of kills.'
Then I thought:

If God has forgiven all the sins that I have committed,
can't I allow a hornet one error of judgement
without making it pay with its life?
Maybe I can't rescue and rear an orphaned orang-utan,
but I can save hornets.
So I kept a plastic cup and piece of cardboard
on the microwave,
and when a hornet landed on a wall
I popped the cup on top of it,
slid the cardboard underneath,
took it out to the garden
and released it.
So don't say you never learn anything useful in church.
You now know how to deal with invading hornets.

Brian Ford

A DIFFERENT MOTH POEM

Night-flying?
Battering light bulbs?
Dying in candle flames?
Scattering impassioned
metaphor?

No way!

Day-dancing, darting
above valerian's pink,
a blur, a whirr of russet wing,
furry bug-body bopping,
dropping, dipping,
probing the pinkness, sipping
(proboscis swift as light and
microchip-precise) –

hummingbird hawk-moth

transfiguring
a human day.

Eleanor Nesbitt

ALL THE LOCAL MOTHS

Knit one, purl one,
knit one, purl one,
this one's going to be so good;
the best I've made so far.

But I thought hand-knit was so yesterday,
so last decade, so last century.
Buy cheap synthetic
and throw away, I say!

Shh ... Knit one, purl one,
knit one ...
Nah, it's all back in fashion again.
This one will blow them away,
they'll all be green with envy;
hand knitting is the next big thing.

What a lot of work
when you could be down to town and back
with something just as good
in less than an hour.
Buy cheap synthetic
and throw away, I say!

Sh ... Sh ... Knit one, purl one,
knit one, purl one ...
It's so satisfying
creating it myself,
and in real wool – you don't get that nowadays.
God made us creative:
He wants us to use our imaginations,
our hands, our gifts.

Buy cheap synthetic
and throw away, I say!
But at least, doing it yourself,
you're helping God's creatures.
All the local moths are thanking God for you
and your generous gift to them.

Huh?! Huh? ...
Knit one, purl one,

knit one – bother, I've dropped a stitch.
It's run all the way down.
Bother, bother, bother!
Perhaps I won't bother after all.

Meet you at the shops tomorrow?

Carolyn Morris

NATIONAL INSECT WEEK

Spiders in the bathroom
run to God

bluebottles in the kitchen
buzz to God

daddy longlegs in the bedroom
dance to God

beetles under the skirting
crawl to God

silverfish in the pantry
slither to God

moths against the windows
flap to God

worms that the cat brought in
wriggle to God

God's wee creatures
all over my house
bring God glory.

Ruth Burgess

EVERYBODY KNOWS THAT CATS LIKE TO RUMBA

Eels like to shimmy
and cows do a hoedown
rhinos hornpipe and
hippos can hula
but everybody knows that cats like to rumba

Pollywogs can cakewalk
flamingos can cancan
dingos tango
peacocks fandango
mongooseys watusi
and wapitis dance boppity
but everybody knows that cats like to rumba
everybody knows that cats like to rumba

Mambas mambo
molluscs mazurka
llamas samba and
pandas La Bamba
Wonga-wongas like to conga conga
but everybody knows that cats like to rumba

Foxes like a trot
German shepherds polka
bunnies bunny hop
bugs like to jitter
ducks disco
swordfish sword dance
tapirs caper and civets
and vervets curvet
but everybody knows that cats like to rumba

Chimps do the monkey
worms do the worm
wombats do the wild wildebeest
shaggy horses clog dance
polar bears like a snowball
hairy black spiders tarantella
but everybody knows that cats like to rumba

Emus and gnus boogaloo
rattlesnakes shake their bootys
bees do the honey dance
bears are chained to waltzes
svelte silky impalas saraband
colourful coral fish calypso
but everybody knows that cats like to rumba

Giraffes gavotte and
guinea pigs dance the Irish gig
lambs do the fling in spring
whales ballet
newborn things do the hokey-cokey
but everybody knows that cats like to rumba
everybody knows that cats like to rumba

Camels do the bump bump bump
skunks are full of funk funk funk
amoebas pair off
boas hold their last dance close
stinkbugs cut a mean rug
porcupines dance alone mostly
whelks and elks got nothing in common much
but everybody knows that cats like to rumba

Lemmings mosh and
drakes do a slam dance
beetles twist and shout and shake it up baby now
but everybody knows that cats like to rumba

Gypsy moths dance by caravan light
Shetland ponies like a ceilidh
baboons ballroom and
ants like a march tune
centipedes have to be careful and
millipedes have to be carefuller
but everybody knows that cats like to rumba
everybody knows that cats like to rumba
everybody knows that cats like to rimba, rumba, roo!

Neil Paynter

OUCH!

Ouch!
God,
why did you create midges?
And even if you made a mistake,
why did you let them onto the ark?
Or maybe you didn't,
maybe they just hung around in the air
waiting for fresh blood to come out on deck!

Ouch!
It's not too late to do something, God.
I don't think anyone would be too upset
if midges suddenly turned cannibal
and ate each other up overnight.
Though, on second thought,
that might create a new breed of giant midges!
Forget that suggestion please.

Ouch!
I get this nasty feeling that the midges
are listening in to this conversation,
and they're not impressed.
They reckon they have as much right to
your love and protection as I do,
and they could be right.

Ouch!
Sorry, midges,
maybe extinction was a bit extreme.
I still have no idea why God created you,
but I'm not going to hang around here any longer
or ask any more questions.

Ouch!
Sorry, God,
time to go.
Goodbye.

Ruth Burgess

ENVIRONMENT

A HYMN FOR WORLD ENVIRONMENT DAY

(Tune: Sine nomine)

Creator God, abundant life your mark,
you once poured speech into the formless dark;
and from those words sprang forth a living spark.
Your inspiration
awoke creation.

And so this world, in which we live and move,
all that we sense below, around, above,
displays the imprint of your longing love:
its revelation
throughout creation.

But yet the earth is fractured, frayed and torn,
poisoned, polluted, ravaged, scarred and worn,
its treasures plundered and its beauties scorned:
our desecration
of God's creation.

From blight and guilt, we cannot walk away,
our will and actions shape the world today;
and ours the greed, insistent on its way,
whose depredations
despoil creation.

Come Holy Spirit, challenge mind and heart!
Inspire our living so that we can start
to make those choices which may yet impart
love's liberation
to your creation.

We pledge to touch all things with holy care
until your coming Kingdom ends despair:
when all the world will witness and will share
the jubilation
of healed creation.

Pat Bennett

OUR FOOTPRINTS ARE HEAVY

God our creator and healer,
we confess that we have sinned:
we have used creation
not cherished it;
we have lived selfishly,
not watched the balance of life;
we have been greedy
not sharing earth's gifts;
and our footprints are heavy
not gentle.

Forgive us the damage
that disturbs our planet.
Grant us the grace
to live for the world's healing
and our own.
Bless the seasons of the year –
may they be restored
to your design.

Chris Polhill

TWO QUESTIONS

Dear God,
What vitamin did you put in water
to make plants and flowers grow?

Dear God,
Can you stop rain
in Tyne and Wear?

Peter, aged 8; Marie, aged 7

OUR POLLUTED WORLD

Amazing God, we pray for our polluted world.
We know not to dump chemical and nuclear waste
but we compromise our natural instinct and awareness
by dumping toxic rubbish in hidden-away places,
places like the sea
or deep within our sacred earth.

God, stop us –
this behaviour is crazy
and an insult to ourselves and you.

Loving God, lead us from living like resource-guzzling parasites
to being able to live more harmoniously within creation.

Creative and dynamic God, this is your world.
We are willing to live simply and to find better, less toxic ways.
God, enable us.

Simon de Voil

BE WITH ME, GOD

A personal prayer for World Oceans Day

Be with me, God,
in all the sea changes
of my life:

When I'm drifting in the doldrums,
let me rest in you,
rather than wearing myself out,
straining at the oars of half-belief.

When undercurrents of irritation
drag me off course,
hold the helm firmly –
your strong hand guiding mine.

When the squalls and storms
of daily living
threaten to capsize me,
still me with your peace.

When I'm fearful
in the fog banks of uncertainty,
help me discern the way to go.

When I wallow in the depths of discontent,
sickened by my dissatisfaction with life,
revive me with your joy.

And when all is well in my world,
as I skim across the crest of faith
enjoying the exhilaration of your love,
ride the waves with me, so together,
we surf the seaboards of eternity.

Carol Dixon

FORGIVE US

For the reservoirs that drowned people's homes:
FORGIVE US, LORD.

For wasting water without thought:
FORGIVE US, LORD.

For the many who still have only dirty water to drink:
FORGIVE US, LORD.

For forgetting that water is a gift:
FORGIVE US, LORD.

Bless those who will have to carry water to their homes.
Today, and every day,
may we treasure each drop of water. Amen

Chris Polhill

RAIN

Dear God,
How does the rain come down?
Do you squeeze a cloud, and is it like a dishcloth to you?

Joseph, aged 8

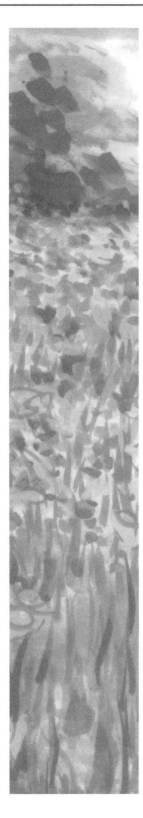

ISLAND PRAYER

When God does not speak
perhaps the island will,
for I want to be still
and feel the earth beneath my feet
and hear the waves lap on the beach.

When God does not speak
perhaps the island will,
for I want to be still
and feel the breeze touch my skin
and hear the pipits sing.

When God does not speak
perhaps the island will,
for I want to be still
and look far out to sea
and let it speak to me.

Elizabeth Baxter

FIRM IS THE ROCK

Firm is the rock
unmoved from generation to generation:
LORD, WE PRAISE YOU FOR YOUR FAITHFULNESS.

Hard is the rock
born from the heart of the earth:
LORD, WE PRAISE YOU FOR YOUR MAJESTY.

Warm is the rock
heated by the sun's rays:
LORD, WE PRAISE YOU FOR YOUR LOVE.

Enduring is the rock
resisting the wind and rain:
LORD, WE PRAISE YOU FOR YOUR PATIENCE.

Sturdy is the rock
standing tall above the moor:
LORD, WE PRAISE YOU FOR YOUR STRENGTH.

Great is the rock
sheltering all from storm and gale:
LORD, WE PRAISE YOU FOR YOUR CARE.

Simon Taylor

IN THE BEGINNING

In the beginning, God created the heavens and the earth,
and the Spirit of God breathed life into being,
and it was all very good in God's eyes.
Let us bless the Lord:
THANKS BE TO GOD.

A potted plant is placed on a central table.

In the beginning was the Word,
with God, the same as God,
and by him all things were created.
Let us bless the Lord:
THANKS BE TO GOD.

An open bible is placed on the table.

And the Word became flesh and dwelt among us,
and we have seen his glory,
the glory of the Father's only Son.
Let us bless the Lord:
THANKS BE TO GOD.

A lighted candle is placed on the table.

Jesus is the image of the invisible God, the first-born of all creation,
and through his cross all things on earth and in heaven
are reconciled to God.
Let us bless the Lord:
THANKS BE TO GOD.

A cross is placed on the table.

David Hamflett

GARDEN GATHERING

In the stillness of this garden
we are held
in this moment
together

with eyes to see beauty,
ears to hear distant sounds,
feet to touch the ground beneath us.

We taste the wild strawberry,
and smell lavender.
We are called forth to delight.

Gentle God of gentle earth,
you invite us to behold your wonders,
you beckon us to step into your embrace,
you caress us with acceptance.

We dare to respond,
tiptoeing with awe,
feeling our way
into your abundance,
laughing with the breezes,
engaging with your generosity.

Elizabeth Baxter

BREATHING CIRCLES

I'm thinking of the future, I'm thinking of the past:
one will never ever be, the other's been surpassed.
I've seen the life force come; I've seen the life force go;
with clenched fists I have tried in vain to change the status quo.
The world just keeps on turning, winter turns to spring;
I keep getting older, I still try to cling
to worthless dreams of permanence, feeding on a flight
of my imagination that day won't turn to night.
And when I'm sick of being sick of this imagination,
I watch my breath go in and out, its own determination.
We're given a breath; we give it back, a thousand times an hour,
then it's mixed with sunlight and fed to every flower,

and in that breath a circle turns, without a start or end:
the past and future overwhelmed, and with the moment blend.

Stuart Barrie

TEACH US TO CARE

Lord, we thank you for the earth
which mothers us, feeds us, clothes us, shelters us.

For air to breathe
THANK YOU, LORD
For water to drink
THANK YOU, LORD
For food to eat
THANK YOU, LORD
For shelter and warmth
THANK YOU, LORD
For beauty and fun
THANK YOU, LORD

Forgive us that we are careless with the earth,
polluting and harming it.

For hill, field and wood
TEACH US TO CARE
For river, lake and sea
TEACH US TO CARE
For bird, animal and fish
TEACH US TO CARE
For flower, bush and tree
TEACH US TO CARE

Teach us to care, as you care. AMEN

Simon Taylor

JOURNEY AND PILGRIMAGE

THE JOURNEY

Lord Christ,
I know not where this journey will lead,
but you do not leave me
unguided:
Thank you for those
whose lives, by word, deed and example,
have become
a signpost for me.

Lord Christ,
I know not where this journey will lead,
but you do not leave me
in solitary joy:
Thank you for those
whose lives have overflowed
to mingle with mine
in the celebration of your love.

Lord Christ,
I know not where this journey will lead,
but you do not leave me
uncomforted:
Thank you for those
who, in love and compassion,
have met me in my brokenness
and brought healing.

Lord Christ,
I know not where this journey will lead,
but you do not leave me
unsheltered:
Thank you for those
who, with warmth and generosity,
have made their lives
places of 'home' for me.

Lord Christ,
I know not where this journey will lead,
but you do not leave me
unchallenged:

Thank you for those
whose words and questions
have stretched me and sent me out
to search for you.

Lord Christ,
I know not where this journey will lead,
but you do not leave me
to walk alone:
Thank you for those
who, in the sharing of their lives,
have become
my companions of the way.

Lord Christ,
we know not where this journey will lead,
but it is enough
that you are its beginning
and its end,
and that you travel
with us.

Pat Bennett

JOURNEY HAIKUS

High tide brings the fruits
which sustain life's journeyer
when the ebb tide runs

Only in valleys
do the mountaintop visions
yield up their riches

Pat Bennett

PILGRIMAGE

'There's no discouragement
shall make him once relent
his first avowed intent to be a pilgrim.' John Bunyan

A what?
Sounds very high church,
pretty doubtful really;
an example of extremism,
fanaticism ...

I'm moderate,
measured,
middle of the road,
sound. Yes, sound.
I certainly don't believe in shrines
and walking barefoot 'til your feet blister.

And look at the lot who travelled through the pages of Chaucer to Canterbury –
hypocritical, greedy, immoral.
Pilgrimage is a hotbed, a breeding ground for trouble.
So unsuitable
for moderate, measured, middle-of-the-road me.

But
where are *you* going?
What are *you* seeking?
Are you sure it's safe, and sound ... and sound?
I'd quite like to travel on as well:
it's not quite my 'avowed intent'
but maybe I'll take a step or two.

Only
let's not call it pilgrimage.
It's just a journey,
my journey.
And I'm seeking,
going towards ...
but keeping in the middle of the road,
just in case!

Carolyn Morris

BLESSING

For the Iona pilgrimage on Saint Columba's Day

Here, find surging pebbles
in ceaseless torn streams,
speckled and worn
from hollows of the sea.

Here, pluck one sloe berry
of the shore
and place it on a cairn.

Here, lay your fears
to rest.

Mary Palmer

ARISE WITHIN ME

Arise within me, Holy mystery, Holy friend

keep danger near enough for the summoning of protection
keep doubt strong enough for the deepening of trust
keep despair near enough for the stirring of hope
keep darkness strong enough for the glimmering of light
keep hostility near enough for the sustaining of peace
keep fear strong enough for the arousing of love
keep greed near enough for the lavishing of generosity
keep uncertainty strong enough for the bolstering of courage
keep surprise near enough for the gifting of grace
keep chaos strong enough for the flowering of creativity
keep divinity near enough for the perfecting of humanity

Arise within me, Holy mystery, take me to hallowed ground.

Carolyn Smyth

HEELING OVER

The sail flapped loose, then curved taut and strong;
cupping the wind, powering the surge,
winging us over the wide dark sea
far from safety and home shoreline.

Slicing through time's wake to now,
I'd thought you the helmsman;
but I was the one steering close to the wind,
trusting in luck and your lodestar.

Lesley Mitchinson

GOD OF OUR JOURNEYING

God of our journeying,
inviting us to travel with you,
forgive us when we cling to outworn security,
afraid to let go of what is safe and familiar.

Give us courage
to take the risk
of answering your call
into joyous adventure.

Jan Berry

LETTER HOME FROM AFRICA

(Benin, West Africa)

… It's amazing the way people here dress in such beautiful, bright colours! Market women in kerchiefs and colourful pagnes (long wrap-around skirts) selling piles of ripe mangos, oranges, bananas, red onions, tomatoes … Beautiful, ebony women swathed in such deep, rich, infinite colour – indigo, turquoise, ultramarine, French blue, ruby, wine, crimson, copper, coral, terracotta, rust, lemon, canary, amber, ochre, saffron …

A woman in a vibrant green pagne: Green as the pyramid of unripe oranges she balances on a tray on her head; green as the sound of a family of parrots sharing a rattan-wicker cage; green as piles of corn husks on the red-brown earth; green as the puddles of truck effluent she steps around, head held high.

Men sometimes wear a 'costume' called a 'grand boubou', which is a robe-like garment with pants and a shirt underneath – some patterns geometric; others kaleidoscopic; some all flowery or leafy; others covered in whorls and spirals; others swimming all over with stylised fish, coral, wavy sea plants …

Some grand boubous intricately and richly embroidered with gold thread around the neck and big sleeves.

Some simply one, solid colour – it depends on the occasion. A man in a solid-blue grand boubou. Like the ocean on a motorbike.

Amazing! All of this colour and design against the background of a grim, ugly city – rotting piles of garbage, malarial mud, rusty tin shacks, hoardings for undertakers, thick black clouds of carbon monoxide choking everyone, dulling everything.

The infinite colours and patterns – the reflection of a rich culture, a fertile imagination, a deeply rooted connection to the land and sea; a land that, by the minute, is being cleared of trees (palms, acacias, baobabs) to supply people with some charcoal to cook over; a spot of warmth against the (surprisingly) cold night. You can smell the bush fires when the wind is blowing a certain way – like the acrid, smoky breath of an apocalyptic beast who brings desert, lumbering closer and closer.

The infinite colours and design – the reflection of the spirit of a people who cannot be crushed – not by slavery, not by colonialism, not by the brutal structural 'adjustment' programmes of the World Bank and IMF … There is an incredible resilience to people here. An irrepressible sense of fun and humour in the ways the children and gossiping market women tease me. An aristocratic dignity, and fierce proudness, in the high-boned faces of burdened women stepping elegantly around raw sewage and truck effluent.

I am a white man – white as enriched, imported French flour; I am respected for my money, knowledge, experience … I am not rich. I am not wise. I am not developed: secure in my first-world privilege, locked in my Land Rover, protected by my mefloquine, bottled water, credit card, open ticket … What experience do I possess of living with death every day, of creative survival, of incredible good-humoured patience, of real hope, of dazzling resurrection?

I feel like a child here. What do I have to teach these people? I have the world to learn from them! …

Neil Paynter

THIS ISLAND OF IONA

God,
we thank you for this island of Iona:
for the newness of its light,
for its shores and sea creatures,
for its tides and fishing boats, farms and birds,
for winds and starlight, misty days, rain and rainbows.
We thank you that Iona gives us
such a powerful sense of your larger creation.
With deep respect and great humility
help us to find our place
within all that you have made.

Martin Hayden, a volunteer on Iona

IONA DANCE

Somehow the air seems to dance differently here,
executing a perfect back-flip into the arms of the short-cropped hillsides,
gliding in sequined splendour and perfect three-four time
across the machair,
juggling with rooks and tossing them ragged,
into the raw wind,
swaying, arms entwined, with the green flags
and the surprised white daisies,
somersaulting spectacularly over the cotton grass,
jitterbugging with the spray and
jiving with the spinning sun-specks
over the water,
tapping in time with the tip-tapping pebbles
as they partner the dinner-jacketed oyster-catchers,
line dancing on the telephone wires
to the hum of other people's messages,
smooching in a long, last waltz with the silver sands ...
somehow, here, the air just dances.

Alix Brown

ON THE BEACH AT ABERDARON

Modern-day pilgrims arriving by car,
with bucket and spade and money
for a mid-morning cake and a cappuccino,
a postcard and a commemorative mug.
Arriving in this timeless place
where the sea meets the sky
and time and eternity
kiss each other.

Modern-day pilgrims arriving as thousands have before,
to cross the threshold of St Hywyn's Church,
to enter the peace of heaven on earth
and join their prayers with the prayers of the saints,
accompanied by the sea and the wind
and the sound of the seagull crying.

Modern-day pilgrims mark fresh-washed sand,
until the washing of time and tide
removes their mark,
and reminds us
of our ephemeral encounter with this place,
where fresh-washed stones
and the sea and the wind
bind prayer to the truth of eternity.

Anne Lawson

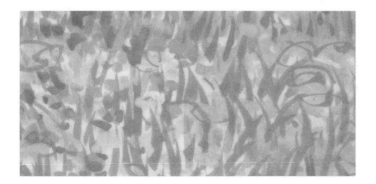

AFFIRMATION

We believe in God
the maker and shaper of our pathways;
who sent Jesus to show us the narrow way,
and who is the beginning and end of our travelling.

We believe in Jesus Christ
the sharer of our flesh;
who entered and experienced the human journey,
and who walks beside us on the road.

We believe in the Holy Spirit
the midwife and nurturer of our potential;
who drove Jesus out into the desert,
and who calls us now to cast off from the shore.

We believe in Father, Son and Spirit
the shaper, sharer and stirrer of our journeys;
and we recommit ourselves
to following their Way.

Pat Bennett

WALSINGHAM

Here, on stones hallowed by pilgrims,
barefoot kings have walked, and martyrs.

Poppies blow across oak and elm
where monks spoke
of mother earth and brother air.

The wells pool water and prayer,
for here lepers were healed.

Now, though fields
are yellow with rape
and the angels bruised,
their faces burnt by acid

still, here
our thirst is quenched.

Mary Palmer

EMPTY CHURCH, WEST SUTHERLAND

It's not locked. When you enter
what you notice first is cool air.
The smell of wood polish
talks to you of unpeopled space.

The floor is made of planks.
Look – see the marks
around each nail's head
the joiner made when he nailed it dead.

The precentor's lectern
stands apart and alone.
White gloves draped
hang by their own weight.

The ladder you see leads to the pulpit.
If some quiet person is seated
there – you won't know.
Be your own master. Up you go.

Beams of light stream in,
gleaming on the wings
of insects that make their way
past dust motes in the air.

You're alone. This is a rare moment.
Be still. Take it in.
Feel the absences,
the presences of quiet places.

Robert Davidson

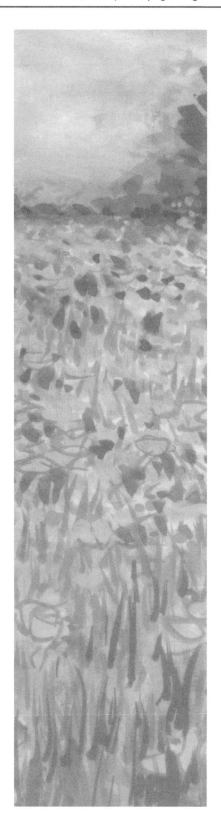

PILGRIMAGE

(Tune: St Columba)

We draw apart from busy life
to set aside some space
and see afresh with open eyes
the beauty of this place.

We glimpse each separate grain of sand,
gold glistening on the shore,
and hear the haunting seagull's cry
above the breakers' roar.

Each quivering blade of grass reveals
the glory of God's earth;
in laughter's lilt, compassion's tear,
the Spirit brings new birth.

We join with all creation's choir
and sing of God's domain,
the love of Christ in empty hearts
now raised to life again.

Refreshed in body, mind and soul,
we return to daily round,
our eyes and ears attuned to God
to serve with love new found.

Carol Dixon

Written after visiting Iona for the first time

FROM A YOUTH FESTIVAL SERVICE OF WELCOME ON IONA

Reading: Matthew 14:13–21

Jesus hanging out with lots of people eating food. Sounds like community to me. There are lots of stories like this one.

I live here in community: I eat soup and home-made bread every day with 70-odd other people. I work in a team with people, I live in a building with about 60 other people, and I meet about 100 new people every week. And I've been here for 19 months now: that's a lot of people. I get a bit peopled-out to be honest – so why do I choose to live here getting paid 75 quid a week? Why do we live in community on this holy island with so many other people? Why not ignore the people aspect and meditate all morning, and then plan actions for justice and peace in the afternoon while walking around this beautiful holy place? The soup and scones can stay but definitely with less people!

It's within the people that the magic happens: the love, friendship, compassion, self-lessness, maturity, caring, brilliance, forgiveness – the transformations. It's in the people that I can most clearly feel and see God and notice how purposeful and miraculous that life can be.

Jesus sounds to me like he was a people person. He talked a lot about God and our neighbours. He related to God in close, people terms rather than in the abstract and wafty way our culture sometimes does: infinite, universal, source of pure and ceaseless light. He just said 'Father God'.

People followed him everywhere, flocking after him, and probably bugged him crazy half the time. They loved him and he loved them.

It's very clear in his teachings: God is in me and you and we need to look out for each other.

So we – this random bunch of people sitting in this church sharing this island – are neighbours for the week, or at least till tomorrow, as there are no more ferries leaving tonight! So let's take this special time together on Iona to be open and caring towards one another. Friendship and kindness are more precious than any gold; they are of love and Love is of God.

Prayer

Loving God, we give thanks to you for this special island and for our time here. Watch over those we've left behind, and be with those who are not warm or welcomed tonight.

Lord, we pray for people who do not have a home, perhaps because of poverty or war. We remember this is a wild world and that you are not a fluffy God. We ask you to care for us and for all of humanity. We ask you to help us care for each other a bit better than we currently do.

Loving and laughing God, we ask you to bless everyone who helps keep the peace and those who bring together warring nations, gangs and families.

May we all learn to respect other people, even when it's hard and we find those people unpleasant or annoying. Help us live as healthy communities, loving and caring for ourselves and others. Father and Mother God, thank you for caring about us. Amen

Simon de Voil

ON OUR DAILY JOURNEY

God of our past,
reconcile our brokenness.

God of our future,
renew our faith.

God of the present moment,
reach out and touch us,
and through us,
the lives of all we meet
on our daily journey.

May we be made whole
through the holiness
of God the Father,
the humanity
of Christ the Son,
and the healing power
of the Holy Spirit. Amen

Ruth Bowen

PRAYER

THE PROMISED PRESENCE

(Family group meeting at Connel)

We were gathered in a room;
as it happened, in an upper room,
with a view of the far island hills
over suburban roofs.

How would he come?
Not from the sky,
not carried by angels,
not seeping like a ghost
through the glass and the walls.

He came from the north,
down the road from Barcaldine
where he'd been leaning on the doorpost of a byre
watching as two crofters and a vet
prayed inwardly for a stillborn calf:
each prayer unknown to the other.

He walked onto the Connel Bridge;
entering its criss-cross calligraphy of steel,
still smiling about the gentleness
of the gruff men.
He stopped and leaned over the rail
to look at the falls, like a tourist,
smiling at the way that his father
had known that the most efficient way
of draining a sea loch would have
been boring.
Falls are imperfect but better.

He opened the door –
nothing is locked to him –
and brought his shy invisibility
into the room.
I'm sure that he sat on the floor,
until we finished praying,
and then he stroked the brilliant

clay of the Indian doll
on the coffee table,
before walking on
to another place of prayer.

Rob Walker

HOME

A piece about working in a home for the elderly

I visit Emily in her bedroom. She sits in her chair, with her 'posture pal'. Emily only ever comes out of her room for meals.

'Hello Emily!' I call. 'So how are you today?' …

She sits gazing. Out the window. In at the past. Chants rhythmically at intervals: 'Are-e, Are-e, Are-e, Are-e …' – to stimulate and comfort herself I guess. 'Are-e, Are-e, Are-e …' To help relieve the boredom, the isolation.

I touch her arm … make eye contact.

'Oh, hello,' she says, and smiles. She tells me that she's sitting waiting for Philip to come and take her home. 'Are-e, Are-e, Are-e, Are-e, that's all.'

I ask her who Philip is and she tells me her brother.

'Your little brother?'

'Are-e, Are-e, Are-e … I think so. I want to go home in the worst way. I want to go home in the worst way now.'

'It's hard …'

'Are-e, Are-e, Are-e, Are-e …'

'Is Philip at home?'

'Are-e, Are-e, Are-e, I guess he'd be home now. At the house.'

'… What kind of house? What kind of house is it?'

'Not a big house, but it's a nice house. Are-e, Are-e, Are-e, Are-e, that's all.'

'A nice house.'

'Nice house … Warm … I wanna go to my bed.'

'Warm like your bed?'

'Yes … Are-e, are-e, are-e. Not a lot of rooms but a nice house. Flowers.'

'Flower gardens?'

'Yes … Are-e, Are-e, Are-e, Are-e. It's way out in Hanover. I'm Hanover. It's outside of Hanover. I want to go home in the worst way. I want to go home in the worst way now.'

'To the nice warm house with Philip.'

'Yes … I wish Philip would come and take me home. So, I sit and wait for him to take me. I sit and wait for him. Are-e, Are-e, Are-e, that's all.'

Everyone here longs to go home. Home to their home – their real home. Home to the past. Home to their mother and father. Home to their brothers and sisters. Home to their husbands and wives and children. Home from here, from this place called a home. Home to God. Home to Mother earth.

Alzheimer victims wander up and down the long, narrow hallways, searching for a way out, a way home. All the doors are locked.

'Are-e, Are-e, Are-e, Are-e, that's all.'

Neil Paynter

SOMEDAY

Someday
I would like to learn
how to pray.

Oh
I can hammer words together
to make a nice box
for you to fill
with all I am sure I need,
but I falter
when I try to climb out
of that hole of hopelessness
I find myself in.

I can bring you
my scrapbook filled
with all the stories
of the brokenness of the world,
but the pages
of my dreams, my fears,
my fickle faith
are out in the trash can.

I can race to you
to tattle on
all my friends and neighbours
so you will notice

all the mud-stains
on their lives,
but in my haste
to get to you first
I stumble over
the shadowed secrets
of my heart.

Someday,
I would like to learn
how to pray.

Thom M Shuman

ON WRITING PRAYERS

I pray when I am writing prayers.
I don't know how or why or what.
Just pray –
no words because they've not been written yet.
Just God and me
with time to think
and ponder images and shape and form and style,
and feel a rhythm in my soul that God put there
for me to find.
Just me and God in holy thought.
I pray.
God speaks.
I write.
And prayer is born anew.

Tom Gordon

NON SOLUM ...

(A prayer)

Why should I open my mouth?
To speak what?
Prayers that you knew before
they even became language?
Fears and desires that filled your heart
before they tested mine?
Delights and gratitudes – pale flickerings
to the sunburst of your glory?

And yet ...
I would give out a cry
that reaches to the last place in the universe,
is heard in the loneliest, most barren wilderness
of rock and dust and fiery gas
of nothingness beyond all nothingness.
A cry that seeks the faintest echo,
the first glimpse of a loved one's face
in the farthest distance,
the largest crowd.
The darkest night.
It is the cry of God calling to Godself,
God in the deepest, loneliest place, to God who is
in all time and all place.

I cry out for you, and to you
for all life, to all life.
I cry because I am alive,
and would live.

Why should I open my mind?
My mind has many doors.
And outside each of them, not only,
or maybe not at all,
a Christ with a lamp.
Instead a baying crowd,
some with their thorny crowns and lantern replicas,
some with shining robes and honest faces.
'Read my message', 'Take my card', 'Follow me'.
A hundred deceits, a thousand lost trails,

a myriad of possibilities.

Will I barricade the doors, draw up to the fire
with a few familiar friends, and reminisce?

God, are you in what I know ... or what I don't know?
Are you the fire or the outside?
Is yours the hand of friend or stranger?

I know the guru's answer, I've walked this way before.
But today, I'll stand aside from that
winding and many-branched path.
I'll rest a while on this bench of thankfulness
and praise you, Creator, for your gift of mind
and your minding.

Why should I open my heart?
My heart is neither open nor closed.
It is the belonging of all that I care for;
the receptacle of me,
the cradling of the child in me,
the shelter of my hopes and dreams.

Am I to let these go?
Empty out my shoebox hoard into some abyss?
Let generosity leave me poor,
compassion leave me empty,
empathy leave me in pain,
care exhaust me,
love expose me,
let you occupy me?

Is that my purpose – to be some other me?

And will that heart be open?

Ah! I see it will,
torn by a Roman spear
emptied of all its treasures
so that they can be

mine.

John Polhill

WE APPEAL TO YOU

(1 Thessalonians 5)

Note: Voice 1 reads their part from a large book, which they open at the beginning of the reflection and close, as indicated, at the end. Alternatively, they could read from a scroll that can be unrolled.

Voice 1:   WE APPEAL TO YOU
Voice 2:   Hello, it's Paul writing to us again.
Voice 3:   I wonder what he's got to say this time.

Voice 1:   BROTHERS AND SISTERS
Voice 2:   I like the way he calls us that, makes us feel like family.
Voice 3:   It feels good.

Voice 1:   BE AT PEACE AMONG YOURSELVES
Voice 2:   That's nice, all gentle and peaceful, lovely.
Voice 3:   Like that.

Voice 1:   ADMONISH THE IDLERS
Voice 2:   Idlers! Who's he calling idlers?
Voice 3:   We work hard here. What's he insinuating?
Voice 2:   What a cheek!

Voice 1:   ENCOURAGE THE FAINT-HEARTED
Voice 2:   Well, yes, we could all do with a bit of encouragement sometimes.
Voice 3:   Even if our hearts aren't particularly faint.

Voice 1:   HELP THE WEAK
Voice 2:   We do do that.
Voice 3:   Tho' it would be good if they could try to be a bit stronger sometimes.

Voice 1:   BE PATIENT WITH ALL
Voice 2:   Patient with all? Has he met Mrs Forsythe Jones?
Voice 3:   Or *Mr* Forsythe Jones, come to that?
Voice 2:   They're enough to try the patience of all the saints!

Voice 1:   DO NOT REPAY EVIL FOR EVIL
Voice 3:   Jesus said that, didn't he?
Voice 2:   It's hard. It's tempting to pay people back.
Voice 3:   But it doesn't really help
Voice 2:   But it's still hard.

Voice 1:   SEEK TO DO GOOD TO ONE ANOTHER
Voice 3:   That's more like it.
Voice 2:   We all do that.
Voice 3:   We look after each other well round here.

Voice 1:   SEEK TO DO GOOD TO ONE ANOTHER AND TO ALL
Voice 2:   To all?
Voice 3:   To newcomers?
Voice 2:   To strangers?
Voice 3:   How far does he think our resources will stretch?

Voice 1:   REJOICE ALWAYS
Voice 2:   Always?
Voice 3:   Rejoice when you're sad?
Voice 2:   Rejoice when you're angry or upset?!
Voice 3:   I don't understand that at all.
Voice 2:   Me neither.

Voice 1:   PRAY WITHOUT CEASING
Voice 2:   Well, that's plain daft, if we did that we'd never get anything done, would we?
Voice 3:   I find it hard to pray for five minutes, let alone 'without ceasing'!
Voice 2:   Me, too. But maybe he's really talking about living? Maybe, as Christians, our prayer is about who we are and what we do, all of the time?
Voice 3:   Steady on, you're sounding like a – like a theologian!

Voice 1:   GIVE THANKS IN ALL CIRCUMSTANCES
Voice 2:   That's a bit like 'rejoice always'.
Voice 3:   And just as nonsensical.
Voice 2:   We'll have to think about that one.
Voice 3:   And maybe ask Paul about it when he comes.

Voice 1:   FOR THIS IS THE WILL OF GOD, IN CHRIST JESUS FOR YOU
Voice 2:   Typical Paul, typical preacher: not only am I telling you this, but God's telling it you too.
Voice 3:   And who can argue with that! *(looks at reader, who closes the book, or rolls up the scroll).*

Ruth Burgess

RELAXING

A friend will laugh and tell me
how she nearly didn't make the bus.
A neighbour's dog had got inside her garden,
which put her in a rush.

We share more serious concerns of family, old and young.
I listen first, and then exchange the role.
We talk of art and books and walks
and intimate matters of the soul.

Do I see here a pattern for my prayer?
What's on your mind or what's your joy, dear Lord, today?
I've told you quite a lot about myself, my fears and cares,
now could I listen happily to what you want to say?

Liz Gregory-Smith

AMEN

Some times and places prompt me to pray:
paddling along a beach;
lying on my settee with my cat sat purring on my stomach;
looking at the moon and the stars;
walking barefoot through a field full of buttercups;
sitting in a church, watching the sun shine through coloured glass
and making changing patterns on the stones;
smelling bluebells in woods after it's been raining;
curling up warm and cosy when it's dark and cold outside.

Some times and places prompt me to pray.
Words come joyfully and easy.
Wow! Beautiful! Thank you, God. Amazing! Amen

Ruth Burgess

PRAYER

It's one of those things we know we should do, but which many of us have trouble practising. It's one of those things that some folk seem to have a gift for, while others of us run and hide when asked to do it. It's probably the thing pastors are asked to do most often, and asked about most often by parishioners, strangers, children …

Other than commentaries on the Bible, I probably have more books on prayer than anything else. I've probably gone to more seminars on prayer than any other topic. I probably spend more time working on prayers than sermons. And I still feel like a kindergartner when it comes to prayer!

I struggle with finding the time for prayer; with the place for prayer; with the words for prayer; with the proper attitude for prayer. There are times when I feel like I need to impress God with my verbal prowess, and so use the prayers of some of the great wordsmiths of the Church, only to wonder *were they saying what I was trying to say?*

I've tried all sorts of 'postures' for prayer, from my nose pressed into the carpet, to my knees aching from wooden floors, to my arms growing weary from being stretched out to the heavens. There are those days when I just don't seem to have the energy, or wisdom, or belief to sustain my prayers, and I have to rely on those simple little ones I learned as a child, including, 'Now I lay me down to sleep …'

But I've decided I am going to keep trying, hoping I will make it to the first grade. I will struggle with words, and trust that the Word that became flesh will whisper them into God's ear. I will try to find the time, even when I don't want to or even think that I have any, and will remain confident that the One who created every moment will take the time to hear my soul. I will use my body, my heart, my hands, my feet, my lips, my eyes, my spirit to bring my hopes and dreams, my fears and joys, to the One who created me out of dust and breathed the Spirit of God into me.

I will, as Jesus says, pray without giving up … because if I give up, I don't have a prayer.

Thom M Shuman

TEACH US, LORD CHRIST, TO PRAY

Teach us, Lord Christ, to pray;
you taught your closest friends
that new and living way
which doubt and fear transcends:
        to seek your wise and just commands
        and trust life to your gracious hands.

Your touch has still its power
to startle to new life
relationships made sour
of children, husband, wife:
        in workplace and in neighbourhood
        to turn the evil into good.

You can reach out to bless
the lost and lonely soul,
in sickness and distress
your touch can make life whole;

we turn to you, all incomplete,
and lay our weakness at your feet.

We gamble on your grace,
knowing your entering in
may fond desires displace
a larger gain to win:
        to do your will our lives are sent
        and in that will we'll rest content.

Words: Ian M Fraser. Music: Donald Rennie.

A PRAYER ROOM

We were talking about prayer yesterday during the discussion hour, about forms of prayer, 'tools' we might use, and so on.

I mentioned my dream, that somehow, in some fashion, the church could offer a prayer room for folk. It wouldn't need to be big and it wouldn't need to be fancy – a chair, a table with a bible and a candle would be all the 'furnishings' most folk would need. But it would be solely devoted to prayer.

Not a room where debates are held, or conflicts nurtured. Not a room where decisions are made as we step on people's toes. No, a room where hurts are offered for healing, where discernment is sought, where relationships are made whole.

Not a room which would need to be rearranged (reluctantly) so a few people could pray, but then has to be put back into place (right away!) so a meeting can be held. But a room that might sit empty for days on end, just waiting in silence and hope for someone to need it.

Not a room where cast-off chairs with nicks and chipped paint are stored out of sight, but a room where the outcast can climb up into God's lap and be loved, welcomed, affirmed.

Not a room where boxes filled with dusty files are kept, but a storehouse of silence, of wonder, of awe, of new life.

Not a room where that old, out of tune piano Aunt Sadie gave to the church years ago can be found, but a room where one can climb that hill in Bethlehem where the angels sang on that first Christmas; where one can enter the green pastures protected by the Good Shepherd; where one can look down the road and see our Parent sitting, patiently looking out of the window, longing to catch sight of all us prodigals trudging wearily home.

Wouldn't it be nice if every church had such a room?

Thom M Shuman

I HEARD ...

I heard a story when I was a kid
about Moses,
in a basket
in a river ...
and I wondered
how a baby could grow up
to lead a whole people to freedom.

So, God,
I pray for babies,
that every single one
might grow up
to fulfil their potential
for you.

I heard a story when I was a kid
about David,
with a sling
against Goliath ...
and I wondered
how a boy could stand firm
and face a giant – and win.

So, God,
I pray for young people,
that every single one
might stand firm
against their own giants – and gain a victory
for you.

I heard a story when I was a kid
about Ruth
and her mother-in-law,
and a faithful promise ...
and I wondered
how anyone could be so committed
and go to the ends of the earth for love.

So, God,
I pray for women,
that every single one
might find love and give love

with absolute commitment
for you.

I heard a story when I was a kid
about Solomon
and a baby
and a sword ...
and I wondered
how a man could be so wise
that everyone would remember what he did.

So, God,
I pray for men,
that every single one
might be so clear-thinking
that they are remembered for their wisdom
for you.

I heard a story when I was a kid
about Abram
and a call
to leave home ...
and I wondered
how an old man could be brave enough
to make a new beginning and travel far.

So, God,
I pray for old folk,
that every single one
might still be brave,
and love life, and travel far, each day,
for you.

Tom Gordon

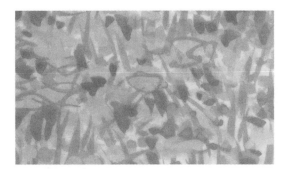

JUSTICE AND PEACE

YOUR CHOICE

(based on Matthew 8:1–4)

If you choose, Lord,
you could wipe out
the poverty in our land

if you choose, Lord,
you could end the suffering
of children and women

if you choose, Lord,
you could destroy all weapons
and institute a reign of peace
throughout the world

if you choose, Lord,
all these things –
and more –
could take place
now.

Lord, like the Hebrews
in the wilderness,
help us to stop our grumbling,
and to remember
you have chosen
to do all these things
through us.

Thom M Shuman

THE COST OF FORGIVENESS

(Matthew 18:21–35)

In speaking the truth,
uncovering lies, deceit and hypocrisy,
give us the courage to name evil.
God of judgement and grace,
HELP US TO FACE THE COST OF FORGIVENESS.

In standing up against evil,
confronting it in others and owning it in ourselves,
give us the strength to pursue justice.
God of judgement and grace,
HELP US TO FACE THE COST OF FORGIVENESS.

In the fulfilment of justice,
repenting wrongdoing and accepting the consequences,
give us the gift of forgiveness.
God of judgement and grace,
HELP US TO FACE THE COST OF FORGIVENESS.

In forgiving and being forgiven,
released from shame and able to begin again,
give us the growth of healing.
God of judgement and grace,
HELP US TO FACE THE COST OF FORGIVENESS.

Jan Berry

THE DREAMS OF CHILDREN

(1 Samuel 2)

God of the displaced,
you weep with those who long for home,
you laugh with those who are united.
Help us to hear your voice
through tears and laughter:
teach us your ways of justice
through the dreams of children. Amen

Elizabeth Baxter

COME, LORD JESUS

Lord Jesus, you are the king who comes in.
You come into the place where we are.
Into our world.
Into our church.
Into our homes.
Into our hearts.

You come as least expected.
You come to unsettle the complacent
and unseat the unjust.
You come whether we want you to come or not.

But this morning/evening, we invite you to come.
Into our world.
Into our church.
Into our homes.
Into our hearts.

Come, Lord Jesus.
COME, LORD JESUS.

Your kingdom is for those who are poor,
and we ask that you would come to the poor today
and give them your wealth.
Come, Lord Jesus.
COME, LORD JESUS.

Your kingdom is for those who mourn,
and we ask that you would come to them today
and give them your comfort.
Come, Lord Jesus.
COME, LORD JESUS.

Your kingdom is for those who are hungry and thirsty
to see justice and right in the world,
and we ask that you would come to them today
and satisfy their longings.
Come, Lord Jesus.
COME, LORD JESUS.

Your kingdom is for those
who are merciful in their dealings with others,

and we ask that you would come to them today
and show them your mercy.
Come, Lord Jesus.
COME, LORD JESUS.

Your kingdom is for the pure in heart,
and we ask that you would come to them today
so that they can see you.
Come, Lord Jesus.
COME, LORD JESUS.

Your kingdom is for the peacemakers
in homes, in churches, in nations,
and we ask that you would come to them today
and reward them with the knowledge
that they are your children.
Come, Lord Jesus.
COME, LORD JESUS.

Your kingdom is for those who suffer
because they stand up for right things,
and we ask that you would come to them today
and give them the kingdom of heaven.
Come, Lord Jesus.
COME, LORD JESUS.

Your kingdom is for those who are insulted
because of their Christian faith,
and we ask that you would come to them today
and give them the knowledge
of their great reward to come.
Come, Lord Jesus.
COME, LORD JESUS.

Come, Lord Jesus, this morning/evening:
to those who are sick and sad – come
to those who are healthy and glad – come
to those taking great decisions – come
to those giving birth – come
to those making music – come
to those making war – come
to those still in bed – come
to those still at work – come.

You are the king
and life holds together when you are here,
so finally we say:
Come, Lord Jesus.
COME, LORD JESUS.

John Davies

A DANGEROUS IDEA

After many years of searching, a man, accompanied by his dog, found himself in a lost city in the middle of a desert. The city contained wealth beyond his imagination. There were ice-blue diamonds as big as eggs, silver plates that sparkled in the sun and gold ingots of deep yellow which stopped his breath and made his eyes bulge. And he thought, *It's true – God will provide.*

He spent the next six days gathering the gold, silver and diamonds into one gigantic pyramid. At the end of each day he sat at the bottom of the growing stack, and smiled and smiled, till he was finally moved to tears. He said to the dog, 'When I was seventeen I fell in love with a beautiful girl, and she felt the same about me … but the joy I felt then does not approach the ecstasy that I feel now.'

'Well,' said the dog, 'I've certainly had your first feeling, but your present rapture is not within my experience.'

'Yes, it's true: money makes the world go round,' said the man.

'I thought it was love?' questioned the dog.

'You stick to chasing cats and leave the philosophy to me.'

The man spent the seventh day in the desert planning his return journey to civilisation. His path would take him to an oasis every night, where he could get water, but since no food was available en route, he would have to carry his rations on his back. The journey would take five days.

The morning to leave dawned. He filled his backpack half with food and half with gold. Striding forth with great purpose, he had not gone a hundred yards, when he stopped, stood still for a moment, then spun round and ran back to his pyramid. He filled his pockets with diamonds, sighed deeply, and started out again. This time he only went fifty yards before he stopped, shook his head, turned and sprinted back once more. He removed half the food from his bag, and replaced it with silver. The dog, who had been sitting silently, watching this performance, cocked his head to one side and said, 'Is that not a bit daft?'

'Don't worry, God will provide,' said the man – stretching his arms towards the sky.

'Nothing is more dangerous than an idea, when it's the only one you have,' the dog replied.

The man looked at him with a puzzled expression. For the third and final time the man set out on his journey, with a heavy heart – and a heavy pack. The dog trotted behind, little realising that the pack contained no food for him. Slowly they wound their way through the dusty day. At evening when the man camped at the oasis and started to eat, the dog asked where his food was.

'Catch a cat if you wish to eat.'

'There are no cats, no rats, no nothing,' pleaded the dog.

'God will provide,' said the man solemnly, tilting his head backwards and looking up at the sky.

The day had been long, the pack had been heavy, his hunger was great. He ate half his food supply that first night. The dog refused to sleep with the man, as was his usual practice, and curled up next to a boulder thinking, *I hope he's cold without me.*

On the second day the man grew tired quickly since he had not slept well. He started eating the food at noon. When they reached the oasis at sunset, he had finished all the food. The dog slept away from him again.

The third day was a great struggle for them both. The hunger was so great the man saw mirages of sizzling sausage and eggs. That night the man tossed and turned. The dog continued to sleep alone.

On the fourth day the man could hardly walk. The heavy pack bit into his shoulders, his legs were weak, his body drained. He staggered, stumbled, and finally crawled on hands and knees to reach the oasis. He lay exhausted; there was only one more day's trek, but he was starving, and could not move another inch. A mirage of roast dog rump started to shimmer in front of him. He propped himself up on one elbow.

'Come and sleep with me,' he pleaded with the dog. The dog sat some distance off and ignored him. He saw a mirage of dog's leg on buttered toast. He offered the dog the diamonds if he would come and be stroked. The dog pretended not to hear. He offered the dog the silver, and finally the gold. But the dog just smiled. The man fell back and moaned. He lay all night getting weaker and weaker. Just before sunrise a frail thought passed through his mind:

I'm dying – at least I'll die wealthy.

As the first rays broke over the horizon he died a very rich, but poor man. The dog, in faint condition, dragged its feeble body over to the man and started to eat. When he was full he lay down and slept. In the evening he awoke, stretched, yawned and ate again. After a refreshing drink from the oasis, he set out at a relaxed run into a soft red sunset … thinking: *He was right, God did provide.*

Stuart Barrie

THE CHURCH IS SENT

The church is sent that it be spent
and God's great love made known:
not just the elect – all can expect
to find God's favour shown.
A church that's sent that it be spent
is nothing on its own.

And yet we long that it be strong,
placed in the highest ranks,
its future need safe guaranteed,
its credit safe in banks –
the motes in neighbours' eyes descried
while in our own are planks.

'We're not to flower through worldly power,'
said Jesus to his band.
To give a guide he shamed their pride
by kneeling, towel in hand,
and made the cross, with all its loss,
a faithful church's brand.

Who for his sake his way will take,
make power the slave of love,

and justice seek for all the meek,
will, as disciples, prove
a church that's spent by grace is lent
a power that mountains move.

Words: Ian M Fraser. Music: Donald Rennie.

EARNING A LIVING

God, watch over us as we attempt to watch over your world.
We pray for people who have learnt to switch off their feelings
in order to have a job and earn a living.
We pray for families and communities where conflict is expected;
where sons are raised to be soldiers.
We pray for those who do jobs that we would not choose to do;
for slaughterhouse employees, for prison guards ...
Watch over us, God, watch over your world.

Simon de Voil

A SOLEMN BLESSING

God has called you to live in integrity and justice.
May you love mercy, act justly and walk humbly with God.
AMEN

Jesus has shown you how to love your enemies and neighbours.
May you seek to be peacemakers and to live in God's light.
AMEN

The Holy Spirit has comforted and disturbed you with God's peace.
May you be full of joy and courage all the moments of your nights and days.
AMEN

May Almighty God bless you:
the Maker and the Son and the Holy Spirit.
AMEN

Ruth Burgess

I BROKE THE RULES

I did not just care for the deserving poor.
I did not just care for the innocent in prison.
I did not just care for those sick through no fault of their own.

I broke the rules.
I broke the rules to back the outcast.
I broke the rules to bear the broken.

I cared, because I loved.
I loved because I am.
I am because I love.

Stuart Barrie

GOD IS GENEROUS

To those without food
GOD IS GENEROUS

To those without work
GOD IS GENEROUS

To those away from home
GOD IS GENEROUS

To those who ask for help
GOD IS GENEROUS

Today, here, where we live,
GOD WANTS TO BE GENEROUS THROUGH US.

Ruth Burgess

A LITANY FOR JOY AND JUSTICE IN SHOPPING

Holy Wisdom,
whose voice calls out in the streets:
WE GIVE THANKS FOR THE LIFE OF THE MARKETPLACE.
Where our daily needs are met
and we discover unexpected gifts and treasures:
WE GIVE THANKS FOR THE LIFE OF THE MARKETPLACE.
Where we learn the value of exchange,
and desire and opportunity meet:
WE GIVE THANKS FOR THE LIFE OF THE MARKETPLACE.
Where we spend what we have worked to earn
and rejoice in what others have made:
WE GIVE THANKS FOR THE LIFE OF THE MARKETPLACE.
For the provision of necessity
and the luxury of choice:
WE GIVE THANKS FOR THE LIFE OF THE MARKETPLACE.
In our dealings, our chat and our gossip,
in the rich exchange of goods and humanity:
WE GIVE THANKS FOR THE LIFE OF THE MARKETPLACE.
Holy Wisdom,
whose voice rings out in the marketplace:
WE GIVE THANKS FOR THE JOY OF BUYING AND SELLING.

For all the times when our desire for a bargain is at the cost of exploiting others:
HOLY WISDOM, GIVE JUSTICE IN THE MARKETPLACE.
For all the times when we grumble at exhausted shop workers on low wages:
HOLY WISDOM, GIVE JUSTICE IN THE MARKETPLACE.
For all the times when our desire for profit cuts corners:
HOLY WISDOM, GIVE JUSTICE IN THE MARKETPLACE.
For all the times when our spending is an empty substitute for what we really desire:
HOLY WISDOM, GIVE JUSTICE IN THE MARKETPLACE.

HOLY WISDOM,
MAY THE COMMON GROUND OF THE MARKETPLACE
BE THE SACRED GROUND OF JUST DEALINGS,
HONEST VALUE
AND JOY IN OUR SHARED HUMANITY. AMEN

Jan Berry

TEACH US TO BE SPARING

(Leviticus 25:1–38; Luke 16:19–31)

Lord Jesus Christ:
teach us to be sparing
that there may be enough for all;
extend us beyond our narrow concepts
that we may be startled by our capacity to give;
and keep us dedicated to our discipline of love
that we may know the painful joy of sharing our riches;
for in your Way lies all our fulfilment
and we need look no further.
Amen

Julie Greenan

THOSE WHO MAKE DO

We give thanks for those who make do on little, Lord God,
making a pittance go far,
ingeniously stretching resources.

We give thanks for those who establish food co-ops
and credit unions,
pointing to the desire of Jesus Christ
that all people might enjoy life abundant;
collaborators with you, the life-sustainer.

The Holy Spirit is at work in our world. Whoopee! Alleluia! Amen

Ian M Fraser

GOD OF THE DIFFERENT WAY

You bless the poor, loving God,
when we wish they would disappear
from our sight (and communities!).

You comfort the grieving,
when we wish they would stop crying
and get on with their lives.

You fill those whose hunger
for your kingdom
will not be filled by platitudes
and whose thirst for justice
is not quenched
by the false promises
of politicians.

You cradle the peacemakers in your lap,
when we would laugh at them
and say, 'Grow up!'

You bless those
we curse
for their idealism,
while you yearn
for the day
we will join
their ranks.

Blessed are you,
God of the different way.

Thom M Shuman

IN TIMES OF CHANGE

NEW BEGINNINGS

Lord, take my life,
my small life,
and illume it:
that everything I say and do
may reflect the light of your glory.

Lord, take my life,
my small life,
and imprint it:
that everything I say and do
may reveal the image of your love.

Lord, take my life,
my small life,
and inspire it:
that everything I say and do
may resonate with the power of your Spirit.

Lord, take my life,
my small life,
and indwell it:
that everything I say and do
may radiate your Life,
your glorious Life.

Pat Bennett

YES

Lord God, help me to discern what you want of my life
and to take your way in the decisions which shape it.
I know that you do not want to control my will
but offer to companion me closely in choices I have to make.
I have only one life to live.
Decisions made cannot be reversed.
So, give me, I pray, your promised companionship,
for you know better than I do what I am made for.
May I hear you say at the end of my days:
'Yes, that is what I wanted of your life.' Amen

Ian M Fraser

IN THIS NEW PLACE

In this new place
may you be blessed in the opening of your doors to the stranger;
may you be filled in the sharing of your bread with the hungry;
may you be enriched in the giving and receiving of love and laughter;

and may the God of grace
gift you with all grace
as you build his kingdom here on earth.

Pat Bennett

ADVENTUROUS GOD

Adventurous God,
you guide our leaps of faith,
our daring to be different.
Please give us the guts
to take it on the chin.
Help us when
all of the above
deserts us.
When the desire to blend in
and not raise a ruckus
or an eyebrow
overwhelms us.

Loving God,
steer us out of our comfort zone
lest it overwhelm us,
and show us the pitfalls
and pratfalls
and dizzy heights
that make up the whole of your world.
Amen

Alma Fritchley

LAST DAY

Dear God,
This morning is our last day to be in the first years.
We go to the second years after the holidays.

Dear God,
This morning is windy and the trees are blowing.
Today it is our last day of term.
We are going to play.

Dear God,
It is the six weeks tomorrow.

Michael, Marie and Philip

HAIKUS ON REACHING SEVENTY

I – the past

I've reached seventy!
Such a rich life behind me,
wealth of memories.

II – the future

I've reached seventy!
Exciting life still calls me
whatever it holds.

III – eternity

I've reached seventy!
Heaven opens wide its gates
welcomes me to God.

Frances Hawkey

THE LONGEST DAY –
THOUGHTS ON RETIREMENT

End of the summer term,
clearing the desk,
listening to the applause
as colleagues raise their glasses
to the completion of a satisfactory and satisfying career –
wishing all good things for the future.

Lasting memories,
unlimited time ahead,
known identity to lay down,
a new image to discover,
other routes to investigate.

Is this the end
of the longest day?
Will the nights draw in and shadows overwhelm,
while the scent and sights of summer
disappear as a mist over mountains?
Will the sun peep out again from silver-lined clouds,
offering rays of comfort and security in an alien landscape?
Will the Son light up the new day as He has done the old?

Autumn's coming;
the days are shortening
but
You and me, Lord,
that's still the same!

Pam Hathorn

TIME OUT*

Leader: God has given you the gift of this time:
Open your hands and your heart
and receive both gift and giver ...

(The person's hands could be anointed at this point and/or between the following stanzas.)

In this time to come, may the Triune God
restore your body, refresh your soul
and re-ignite your hope.

In this time to come, may the Triune God
revitalise your praying, resource your creating
and renew your joy.

In this time to come, may the Triune God
reshape your thinking, rekindle your loving
and remake your living. AMEN

* A prayer for someone about to start a sabbatical, or a personal retreat, or some other time out.

Pat Bennett

LEAVING FOR UNIVERSITY/HIGHER EDUCATION

A time to study and a time to learn about God.
A time for taking responsibility and a time for adult decisions.
A time of hard work and a time for fun.
A time to make new friends and a time to enjoy God's friendship.
A time for discipline and organisation and a time for enjoying freedom.
A time to cook and a time to wash up occasionally!
A time to laugh and a time to share with others.
A time of 'no rules' and a time to decide 'your own rules'.
A time of many challenges and a time of seeing God meet your needs.
A time when difficulties may come and a time to trust God's guidance.
A time to pray and a time to see answered prayer.
A time to grow and a time to discover yourself.

Make the most of your time.

Hilary Allen

STARTING A GAP YEAR

On this 'between-times' journey
may you learn the solace of mountain and desert places.

Through this 'between-times' moment
may your spirit become tuned to God's kairos.

In this 'between-times' place
may you discover and own who and what you really are.

And so may this 'between-times'
become a place
from which you go out
to challenge and change the world.

Pat Bennett

PRAYER FOR A GAP YEAR

O God,

I offer this year
as it opens before me:

Invest its ideas
with your energy;

its events
with your possibilities;

its encounters
with your presence;

that in it
heaven and earth may collide
and your Kingdom come.

Pat Bennett

JOE'S REDEMPTION

Joe had never been popular. He was bright, right enough, and he thought he was considerably better looking than most of the guys his age. And when he mimed to the latest chart hit in front of his wardrobe mirror with a hairbrush ... well, he was simply unbeatable. But he'd never been popular: not one of the in-crowd with the guys, and with no string of girls falling at his feet, he was, he had to admit, a pretty lonely character.

Joe kept himself to himself, believing that he enjoyed his own company, when all the time he really had no choice. That's why he left home when he was seventeen. Well, his brothers and sisters weren't much help. Joe had been a late baby – 'an accident', he'd once heard his mum say – so his three brothers and four sisters were all much older than him, twelve years the gap to the next oldest. And, anyway, he'd probably have better luck somewhere else, where his style and looks might be better appreciated.

It didn't take Joe long to make it big. It was modelling that did it, his young good looks starting him off on small photo shoots, with more and more work coming his way. By the time he was coming up for twenty-one, Joe was the hottest property in the modelling world.

That's when he started getting the letters. The first was from his oldest sister. (How she'd found out his address, he never discovered – but he sure would have been happier if she hadn't!) She'd wanted to get in touch, suggesting that he might be able to 'help her out' of some financial difficulty. The letter was filed under 'wastepaper basket'. The next was from one of his brothers. The tone and content were pretty much the same. He binned that one too. Once a month or so he'd get a letter from someone, mostly family, sometimes an 'old friend'. They all wanted him to help them in some way or another. 'Why should I help them when they did nothing for me?' he would say. Each letter was read and discarded. He never replied to any of them.

Until, that is, one letter told him his father was very sick. 'You should come quickly...' it read. And so he did, making his way back home with considerable apprehension. After all, there would be clear animosity from his siblings. Everyone would know he'd rejected their pleas for help. Everyone would know how selfish he'd been. Everyone would hate him, wouldn't they?

His father died before he got home. The whole family was gathered in his dad's house when he got there. He would not have been surprised if they'd sent him packing. But they didn't. For instead of bitterness, there was an amazing welcome. Instead of hate, there were hugs all round. Instead of recriminations, there was warmth and love.

Joe had never been popular. But he was bright enough to know a new beginning when it was staring him the face, and redemption when it could have its way.

Tom Gordon

GOD WHO STANDS BEYOND THE FUTURE

(Tune: Blaenwern)

God, eternal and unchanging,
though unbound by time or place,
yet with constant, tender yearning
you sustain our human race.
History in all its colours,
present moment where we stand,
hidden future, still to open –
all are gathered in your hand.

God, who sees all human stories,
you in each your touch display;
sometimes known and sometimes hidden
you have met us on our way.
Though we may have failed or faltered,
doubted love, resisted grace,
yet, persistent, you walked with us,
as we travelled to this place.

God, whose life pervades each moment,
meet us in this present hour,
as we open thought and action
to your life's transforming power.
Startle, challenge and confront us,
touch our hearts and free our hands
so that we may see and serve you,
yield to all your love demands.

God who stands beyond the future,
what's to come is still unknown.
Yet, unchanging, you are with us
and we will not walk alone.
Go with us through doubt and darkness,
stand with us in hopeful place,
'til the chain of time is broken
and we see you face-to-face.

Pat Bennett

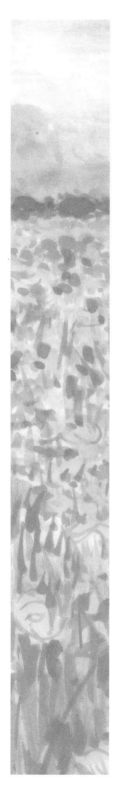

GOD OF NEW BEGINNINGS

(Amos 4:1–8, 12–13; Matthew 15:1–9)

God of new beginnings:
we close our ears to prophetic voices,
and do blind violence,
choked with pride in our own wisdom.
Give us the necessary humility
to strip away all that shrouds
the stark beauty of your truth;
and fill us with courage,
that we may live the way of the heart.
Through Jesus, our brother.
Amen

Julie Greenan

AVOIDING MAKING DECISIONS – THE SEVEN GOLDEN RULES

1. I'll go for it, and if I'm not meant to do it, God will stop me.
That's a good one:
lets me off the hook
and maintains an air of piety.

2. I'll write down all the pros and cons and then decide.
How come my reasons fit neither column
and develop a 'maybe' list of their own?

3. A trouble shared is a trouble halved.
That's OK, as long as I choose to talk to the friends who I know
will agree with me, and give me the advice I want to hear.

4. Take it to the Lord in prayer.
But I'm not too sure that God behaves like a Lord,
and I'm always relieved when the answers don't seem to appear.

5. Time will tell.
Well, it will tell something, whether I decide or not.

6. Sitting on the fence allows me to see both sides.
So true;

and if danger approaches
I can choose which side to jump down on ...

7. If I leave it long enough someone else will decide for me.
Then I can spend the rest of my life
complaining about my lack of choice.

Ruth Burgess

GOD OF TIME AND ETERNITY

God of time and eternity,
be with me in new beginnings
when I am vulnerable and afraid;
protect and enfold me.

God of heaven and earth,
be with me in the continuing
when I am pressured and frustrated;
let me go forward in confidence and strength.

God of joy and sorrow,
be with me in the endings
when I need closure and cannot let go;
bring me peace and fulfilment.

Lord, have mercy on our beginnings
and save us from the love of novelty alone.

Christ, have mercy on our continuings
that we may patiently bear the setbacks along the way.

Lord, have mercy on our endings
that at the last we may come into your presence rejoicing.

Holy Trinity, give us vision, focus and purpose
in our beginnings, continuings and endings,
for you are the Alpha and Omega of all things.

Terry Garley

Taken from a longer piece: 'Kyrie variations from Trinity (Series 1)'

SPEAK TO ME

Speak to me
About the past.
I can discern no meaning in its tapestry.

Help me
Unravel it,
And weave a future
From untangled threads.

Marlene Finlayson

MORNING AND EVENING

GOD OF THE MORNING

God of the morning.
Wake us up.

Wake us up to wonder.
Wake us up to beauty.
Wake us up to justice.
Wake us up to love.

God of the morning.
Wake us up.
Wake us up good.

Ruth Burgess

WASHING BLESSING

To be said whilst splashing your eyes with water

In the name of the Father –
that I may see with wonder.

In the name of the Son –
that I may see with love.

In the name of the Spirit –
that I may see with joy.

Pamela Whyman

JOY OF OUR MORNINGS

(Tune: Bunessan)

God of creation, Lord of all beauty,
all creatures join in singing your love;
holy compassion, joy of our mornings,
fill us with grace which comes from above.

Christ of the outcast, comfort of mourners,
neighbour to strangers, love without end;
bearer of burdens, grace ever-with-us,
blessing our children, brother and friend.

Spirit of kindness, breath of forgiveness,
faithful companion, just as Christ said;
God's little children gathered together,
drink of salvation, feast on your bread.

Thom M Shuman

GOLD PIECES

Thank you, God, for this morning,
for the opportunity of being amazed by your creation,
in every single way.

Thank you, Lord, for the small gold pieces you planted in our daily life:
a smile, a hug, a singing bird,
a warm shower, a good cup of tea,
a stranger saying 'Hi' on the street,
the touch of raindrops on skin.

Thank you, God, for this morning,
for the opportunity of being amazed by your creation,
in every single way.

Sofia Adrian, a volunteer on Iona and at Camas, 2007

TODAY

Today
may I give and receive love.

Today
may I work for justice.

Today
may I listen and pray.

Today
may I sing God's praises.

Today
may I delight in God's beauty.

Today and every day.

Ruth Burgess

IT IS EVENING

It is evening,

calm us, Lord!

It is evening –
another day
of work, of play, of retirement;
home to escape
in front of the TV,
but the same weary news
threatens to swamp us.

Calm us, Lord,
keep hope near
and despair afar.

It is evening ...
and sitting on the front porch
is our old friend, terror,
waiting to tell us
bedtime stories of war,
of nuclear weapons being built,
of pension plans plundered.

Calm us, Lord,
keep trust near
and nightmares afar.

It is evening ...
and the storms of life
rattle the windows
of our souls
and thunder
through our hearts.

Calm us, Lord,
keep faith near
and fear afar.

Calm us, Lord.

Thom M Shuman

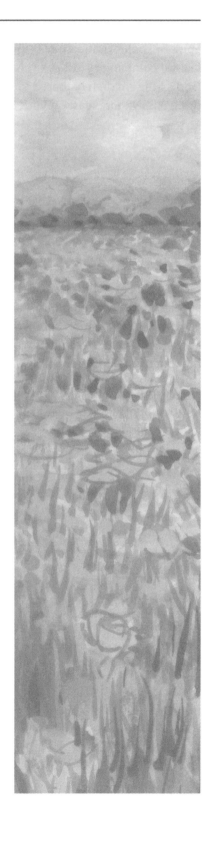

NIGHT PRAYERS

Dear God,
Please can you turn a nightmare
into a dream?

Dear God,
Sometimes I am scared of the dark
so look after me.

Dear God,
I wish I could have a big bed to myself.
If I did I would sleep in all day.

Dear God,
Please protect me at night
because I am frightened.
Can you stop my horrible dream?
I shout out at night.

Dear God,
Please let the night
be safe and nice.

Marie, Tony, Gemma, Jonathan, Candy, aged 7 and 8

GOD OF WONDER

God of wonder and generosity,
bless us this night.
Wrap us round with your glory,
fill our lives with your justice and hope.
May we rest secure,
surrounded by saints and angels.
May we wake to the gift of another new day.

Ruth Burgess

HIDE US IN YOUR LOVE

The mist enfolds the hills in its mantle:
EMBRACE US WITH YOUR LOVE, O LORD

The rain washes the rocks and the leaves:
CLEANSE US WITH YOUR LOVE, O LORD

The stream flows down to the valley:
DIRECT US WITH YOUR LOVE, O LORD

The granite tor stands firm:
ESTABLISH US IN YOUR LOVE, O LORD

The rowan tree clings to the hillside:
ROOT US IN YOUR LOVE, O LORD

The night veils the moor in darkness:
HIDE US IN YOUR LOVE, O LORD

Simon Taylor

I AM TIRED

I am tired, God.
I am ready to sleep.
Let me sleep in your cradling.
Let me rest in your joy.

I give to you my worries.
I give to you my dreams.
Watch over me in blessing.
Watch over me in love.

Ruth Burgess

THE CLOSENESS OF GOD

In the glow of candlelight
amidst the shifting shadows

God folds us
in the soft cloak of eventide

Jesus bids us
to the warm hearth of welcome

The Spirit settles us
with the safe dream of sleep

May the anxieties of the day
leave us

May the fears of the night
leave us

May the closeness of God
leave us feeling beloved.

Elizabeth Baxter

PRAYERS FOR THE WEEK

SUNDAY

Offer your body as a living sacrifice. This is your spiritual worship.
Romans 12:1

Here is my brain, Lord,
my thinking and my imagining.

Here is my face, my self-expression to others,
and my speaking.

Here are my eyes and ears,
my awareness of others and of the world.

Here are my limbs,
with their skills and activities.

Here is my sexuality,
and the heredity I received.

Here is my eating, drinking,
and all bodily pleasure.

Here is my heart, my breathing,
and the wonder of my continued existence.

I am yours, Lord.
Use me as you want.

MONDAY

Seek first the Kingdom of God and his rightness, and all the rest shall be added to you.
Matthew 6:33

Lord, help me to get my priorities right:
my ambitions, and what I hope to achieve this week;
my fears and what I worry about this week.
These I bring before you; help me to get them in the right perspective.
Your Kingdom come –
in me, in my home, in my work, in my community.
Rule in me, do your will in and through me.

Counter all wrongness in me with your rightness,
and empower me to deal with any wrongness.
Your rightness guide me in my dealings with money,
with people at work,
with people in the community and neighbourhood.
So may I achieve something worthwhile in your sight this week,
whatever others may think.

TUESDAY

Rejoice in the Lord, and again I say rejoice! The Lord is near! Be anxious about nothing.
Whatever is true, noble, right, pure, lovely, admirable … think about such things.
Philippians 4:4–8

That is how I would live, Lord, but there is so much in the papers,
on television
and in other places which is horrible, depressing, unclean and frightening.
I bring before you now what I have watched and read.
If I have allowed it to defile or undermine my soul, forgive me.
Teach me when to switch off,
and when to face the world's wrongness and evil in your name.
If I have been escapist, not facing reality,
forgive my weakness;
make me strong in the Lord
that I may face reality undaunted.
I thank you for all which has opened my eyes to wonder in nature
and in human life.
And now, seeing the world's sin and pain in the light of your cross,
may I rise with you,
to rejoice in the love which gives the joy which nothing can take from us.

WEDNESDAY

I believe in God, Father, Son and Holy Spirit.

Some folk believe in communism,
but I believe in you, God.
Some folk lack the self-confidence to believe in themselves.
Never mind self-confidence,
I believe in you, God.
I have no need to hide my weaknesses, or to put on 'a good show',
I believe in you, God.
They say I'll never get anywhere on this basis.
But I believe in you, God.
I may get good luck or bad luck ... so what?
I believe in you, God.
I am a nobody who is the beloved child of God,
a failure Christ is dying to know.
And my body: the temple of the Holy Spirit.
Believe it or not!

I've all sorts of problems –
in me, in my home, in my work.
But I believe in you, God.
Now I am going to live that out to the full – by Christ!

THURSDAY

That you may be filled with all the fullness of God.
Ephesians 3:19

I'm a spent battery –
recharge me!

An empty petrol tank –
fill me up!

A deflated balloon –
breathe into me!

Fill all the odd corners of my life,
especially the non-religious ones.

Soak me through and through
till your goodness runs out of me.

Let my links with other people
be alive with the power of your love.

My dying be filled with the glory
that shines from your face.

FRIDAY

Father, into your hands I commit my life.
Luke 23:46

Into your hands I commit all that is good and creative in my life,
only you can make the most of it.

Into your hands I commit my mistakes,
only you can redeem them, bringing good out of them.

Into your hands I commit my sins,
only your forgiveness is big enough to cover them all.

Into your hands I commit what I do not understand about you,
only you can answer my questions.

Into your hands I commit me.
Over to you.

Now let us just get on with it.

SATURDAY

For me, to live is Christ.
Galatians 2:20

Christ behind me in the past,
treasuring what was good,
redeeming what was not good.
Christ in the future,
guiding me through problem areas,
leading me home safely, in spite of me!
Christ beside me, sharing in every situation:
'I am with you always.'
Christ over me:
'Under the shadow of your wings I am safe.'
Christ beneath me:
'Underneath are the everlasting arms.'
Christ around me,
between me and everybody I am meeting.
Christ in me,
no showing off, no self-assertiveness.
Just letting Christ be in me,
especially
when I am not being 'religious',
not being 'a Christian',
and above all
especially when I don't notice it.
So, Lord,
let's live!

Ian Cowie

DAILY LIFE

A WORKING CREED

I believe that I am made in God's image.
I believe that in Jesus I see God's image lived to perfection.
I believe that
by listening to the promptings of the Spirit,
by following Jesus's example of love and service,
and by making his priorities my own,
I become more in tune with God's image within me
and closer to the person I was made to be.

I believe that I cannot do this if I live in isolation
or surround myself only with those I understand –
but that I must touch the world I find around me
and engage with the people I meet there.

I believe that institutions
are sometimes necessary
but often misleading –
blinding people with their power
or fooling them with an appearance of anonymity.
I believe that there is no such thing as anonymity,
and that every interaction is between people,
who are made in God's image,
who love and suffer and rejoice and weep,
who do their best and sometimes fall short.

I believe that God has placed me in the world
at this moment in time
and that I must do my best to inhabit it beautifully.

Cally Booker

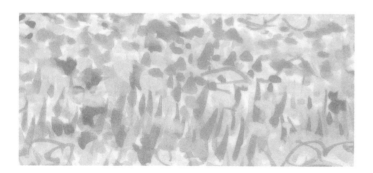

STORYMAKING GOD

(Tune: Abbot's Leigh)

In the stories that surprise us,
when we find the words to tell,
in the meanings that delight us,
with their liberating spell;
in the dawn of hope awaking,
in the wisdom that we find,
God-with-us in storymaking,
speak the words that free our mind.

When our stories grow in spinning,
learning from each other's art,
when each end is a beginning,
and each knot and strand a part;
in the tangled risks we're taking,
in the fragile web we weave,
God-with-us in storymaking,
help us act what we believe.

And when stories can't be spoken,
when the grief cannot be told,
when the threads of trust are broken,
torn apart by terror's hold;
when we're weary with the aching
of the pain we cannot share,
God-with-us in storymaking,
hear the silence of our prayer.

When in symbol, dream and story,
we are searching for what's true,
when in holy human glory
God is making all things new;
in the loaf of bread we're breaking,
in the cup of wine outpoured,
God-with-us in storymaking,
live in us, as flesh and word.

Jan Berry

Written for the Women in Ministry Conference, Windermere, 2005

FRIENDSHIP

God, we give thanks for friendship
and for all the amazing people who love us for who we are.

God, we know that without these people
we would be less loving and less amazing ourselves.

God, we give thanks for friendship. Amen

Simon de Voil

OUR DAYS

Dear God,
I don't like it when it is a dull day.
It rains and the clouds are grey.
Please try to make our days sunny.

Andrew, aged 7

TICKLE ME, GOD!

When I believe
there are no miracles left
(at least, for me)
tickle me
with your grace
till I ache
with life.

Thom M Shuman

SCREAMING INSIDE

I'm screaming inside ...

Look!
Really look!
Look at the real me.
Don't talk to the person you want me to be.
Talk to me.
Listen to what I'm really saying,
not to what you think you hear.

Please ...

Take time with me.
Look deep inside.
Have a care
not to trample on the fragile dreams
you find there.

Accept ...

Me as I am now
and as I am becoming.

And allow me
in my turn
to accept you
the real you ...

who is screaming inside.

Julia Brown

HUSH PUPPIES

A piece about working at a night shelter for homeless men

One night at the shelter, Lee, who's 17, told me about the problem he was having with his new girlfriend:

'It's cause of the abortion, eh. It wasn't my baby. It was the guy before me. He took off out West. Jerk. Or scared, I dunno. So now whenever I try to get close to her she just starts wailin' me in the shins. She's got these big, kick-ass, steel-toed boots – man, it hurts. It's just when she's drinking. I don't know what I'm gonna do. She won't let me near her. And I can understand – I always say to her: "Look, I wanna understand, let me in, let me in on about how you're feelin'" ... But she doesn't believe me. Can't blame her really. I don't know what I'm gonna do. I need my hugs, man.

Then I was walking through the mall the other day, you know, and stopped in front of this store window. And looked in and all of a sudden it came to me – hush puppies, yeah, hush puppies. Shoe store. Hush puppies, get her some hush puppies – soon as my next welfare cheque comes. I need my hugs ... It's only when she's drunk but, man, it hurts – take a look at my shins. See – all bruises ... I'm gonna buy her some hush puppies – soon as my next cheque comes.'

Neil Paynter

PEOPLE RUSH

People rush
to get a bus
to go to work
every day,
to get the money
to buy the food
for the family.

John, aged 8

THE DANCE

Stepping into this moment
we gather together
CELEBRATING A DANCE OF DIVERSITY

Stepping into this space
we bring ourselves
CELEBRATING UNIQUENESS AND OPENNESS

Stepping into this community
we acknowledge the other
CELEBRATING THE PRESENCE OF THE DANCER OF LOVE

Stepping into the dance
others have danced before us
WE CALL THEM TO ACCOMPANY US

Stepping gently on the earth
with friendship and wonder
WE JOIN NEW DANCING PARTNERS

Stepping into a dance
unrehearsed
WE FIND OUR FEET,
OUR FAITH
AND OUR FUTURE.

Elizabeth Baxter

THINGS WE CAN MAKE AND DO

Dear Lord,
Thank you for all the music we can make.
Thank you for things we can do
like read and wright.

Martin, aged 8

THE BIG BOOK

For years I wanted things and things,
security and diamond rings,
recognition, admiration
(I'm only human) and salvation;
to know 'the secret'. Till I found
'the secret' was the thorns that crowned;
that the Kingdom is not hidden,
truth can never be forbidden.
And now and then in morning mist
I am sighted, held and kissed,
the Big Book breaks, the sunlight warms
with cutting rain, dark cleansing storms,
the crow caws hard, the newborn cries;
sweet love is born when my love dies.
God's life dissolves, there's just the lamb,
the silence in the self I am.

Stuart Barrie

THE GOD OF LOST PROPERTY

'Please remember to take with you all your items of luggage and all personal belongings – all newspapers, umbrellas, bad habits, guilty secrets, feelings of worthlessness, frustration, fears and resentments …

'We do hope that you have enjoyed travelling with us and that you continue to have a pleasant journey.'

Dutifully, I gather together my baggage. I have lost nothing, I have left nothing, I am doing well. I have no hands free to open doors, greet, hug, embrace or wave, but I carry on, proud of my ability to maintain so much stuff without losing it.

And out into the roar of the crowd I walk, my sole objective to get from A to B without dropping anything.

In my blinkered determination I am painfully aware that I can't hold on to all these wretched things for much longer.

In head-down hurry I rush on, unseeing until the moment of our inevitable collision.

Like hitting a rock or wall. Shock waves send my luggage flying – bags bursting open as they hit the floor, scattering the contents of my life across the pavement.

I look up in a fury of embarrassment, confronting you face-to-face.

I am met by your gaze of infinite calm and patience.

I want to kick your shins.

'You look as if you have your hands full,' you say.

'It is my property,' I say, 'you made me drop it.'

'I know,' you say. 'It looks heavy. Why not leave it here?'

'But I need it,' I say.

'Do you?' you ask. 'Really?'

I want to gather it all to my chest. I feel naked – vulnerable standing there without it. I am not quite myself.

I go to pick it all up again. But I cannot, I am too tired.

'Will you look after it?' I ask.

'I will take care of it,' you answer. 'Go on – I dare you. Leave it here with me. I promise it will be in good hands.'

I hesitate. I move forwards, light-headed but also suddenly light-hearted.

I walk onwards. I swing my arms, I stride.

It is so easy, so free and easy.

I glance back and all is gone. I look forwards and all is before me.

My property is lost and I am found.

Lisa Debney

I WISH

Dear God,
I wish I had a car in the back garden but dumped.

Dear God,
I wish I could drive now.

Robert, aged 7

WOULD I ASK?

(A hymn to stop you going back after Easter)

Now for everyone who loves and
everyone who fails and
everyone who ran away
and didn't dare look back and
everyone who's blown it,
everyone who's broken,
everyone whose hopes are dashed
and boats are burned!

Chorus: Christ says, 'Brother, do you love me?
I am with you all empowering!
Sister, do you love me?
Would I ask if you were hopeless?
Lover, do you love me?
Take and eat, digest, do justice!
Every debt is written off.
Now live for me.'

All the places we sneak back to,
grooves that we slot into,
every time we shake a head
and say, 'There's nought to do.'
But nothing keeps the risen
Jesus in his prison,
ours his arms of flesh and blood
embrace the world.

Chorus

David Coleman

PRAYER IN UNCERTAINTY

God of those who falter:
give us grace in our uncertainty;
give us courage
to persist in choosing you
over and above all else;
to keep on risking vulnerable love;
to keep on keeping the faith. Amen

Julie Greenan

GOD SENDS US MESSAGES

(Prayers from an all-age service with a computer theme)

Prayer of confession

God sends us messages:
when we receive them God makes our lives better
when we delete them we make our lives worse.

When your message says 'Love others' and we don't
DEAR GOD, WE'RE SORRY.

When your message says 'Love ourselves' and we don't
DEAR GOD, WE'RE SORRY.

When your message says 'Love me' and we don't
DEAR GOD, WE'RE SORRY.
HELP US TO LOVE YOU.
HELP US TO KNOW YOU LOVE US.
HELP US TO SHARE YOUR LOVE WITH OTHERS. AMEN

Words of forgiveness

May God, who is full of love,
forgive you and free you,
heal you and strengthen you,
help you to get the message
and live the new life of Jesus
in the strength of the Spirit. AMEN

Prayers of intercession

*The prayers were done as 'emails': letter E's were cut out of
paper and each member of the congregation was invited to
write their prayer on one. Then the prayers were collected up in
baskets and brought to the front at the offertory. (In another
children's service, the E's were clipped to a line of string across
the hall – thus they went 'online' to God. Corny but effective!)*

Prayer after communion

We have eaten bread together,
we have taken a sip of wine,
we have come and received God's blessing,

we have got the message:
Jesus shows us that God loves us;
the Spirit helps us to live for heaven;
God's plan is complete.
We give thanks.

John Davies

LISTENING GOD

Listening God,
I never really had much hope
for your human race.

We seem at best
silly and outrageous,
at worst,
well, read any paper.

And then, through you,
we go and surprise ourselves –
amaze ourselves –
with spontaneous acts
of kindness.

'Man saves dog from freak wave.'
'Woman frees trapped child from car.'

Thanks for sticking with us, God,
when the going gets tough.
Thanks for taking us through trials
to triumph.

Now,
let us go from joy
into justice
From fear into freedom. Amen

Alma Fritchley

THE IMPORTANCE OF WAITING

I never thought about the importance of waiting.
When time seems to stand still;
when nothing seems to be going anywhere.
Waiting,
for doctors and verdicts,
friends and relatives,
the 'what next?' and 'how will I cope?'.

I never thought about looking at the waiting,
searching for clues to help me be prepared, be ready,
for what is about to come.

I often wondered about praying in the waiting.
But didn't have the words,
thought my despair not worthy.

'Comfort, O comfort my people' says God into our waiting.
'I give you a light,
a light that will shine in the darkness,
and the darkness shall not overcome it.'

I will hold on to hope in my waiting.
Hope that the time of waiting
will pass with peace,
will look forward with a glimpse of joy,
will draw me nearer to the arms of the loving God,
who brings light,
who brings life.

Kareen Lowther

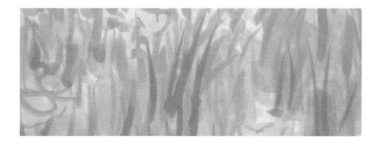

GOD'S PLACE

(Tune: Kingsfold)

O God beyond all boundaries,
you cannot be confined
by Age or moment, form or shape,
by word or creed defined.
And yet you once in human flesh
took root in time and space –
break through the fabric of our lives
and meet us in our place.

Lord, lead us to the inner place
where we may see and own
the things that fetter and distort,
that break our spirit down.
And as we face the dark within
so gift us with your grace,
that in the place of death we find
our resurrection place.

Go with us to the public place
to sound your kairos hour,
to overthrow injustices
and break oppression's power.
Then take us to the place outside
to stand with those alone,
and by our actions and our words
to make our lives their home.

So meet us in that place of hope
where heaven and earth unite,
where doubt and darkness, hate and fear
are scattered by your light.
Then by your life and power transformed
we will reveal your face,
so everything we do and are
will always be your place.

Pat Bennett

RESOURCES FOR
LAMMASTIDE

Lammas Day is celebrated on the 1st of August. In the past on this day in Britain, loaves of bread were baked from the first wheat crop and brought to church to be used as Communion bread. It was celebrated as a day of thanksgiving. The practice died out with the Reformation, and was later redeveloped into the harvest festival.

GOD OF THE RIPE CORN

God of the ripe corn,
on Lammas Day our ancestors
brought you bread
made from the first fruits
of the wheat harvest.

Today we bring you
the fruits of our labours;
our joys and our achievements,
our hopes and our disappointments,
our plans and our dreams.

We ask you to accept
the work of our hands
and our minds
and our hearts.

God of the ripe corn,
bring us safe home
to harvest. Amen

Ruth Burgess

THE FIRST FRUITS

When I bring you the first fruits
you get what you get:
you get my energy,
my imagination,
my scribbling,
my experimentation,
my dreams.
You get the raw me.

Part of me would prefer to bring you
the finished article:
the tried and tested formula,
the buffed and polished carving,
the machine that I know will work.

But that is not what you ask for;
because you want to be with me in the making,
in the messiness,
the uncertainty,
the laughter and the pain.

God of the first fruits,
here I am.
Come and work with me always.

Ruth Burgess

MY BRAVE FATHER

When I started cookery lessons at school,
we took home the fruit of our labours.

My brave father ate his way through:
rock cakes (aptly described),
cheese scones (mostly risen),
jam tarts (only slightly burnt),
mutton stew (brought home in a Kilner jar),
and Victoria sponge (she would not have been amused!).

I imagine you, God,
as equally brave
when you ask for the first fruits of my harvest.

Are you sure
that you wouldn't prefer
me to come back
when I've at least
passed my exams?

Ruth Burgess

FIRST AND LAST FRUITS

God of the first fruits,
let your rain dance on us,
your sun shine on us
and your love and justice grow in us,
until we bring
our last fruits
to your harvest. Amen

Ruth Burgess

GOD OF THE HARVEST

God of the warm earth
ROOT US DEEP

God of the green fields
DRESS US

God of the turning years
BRING US TO FRUIT

God of the harvest
BLESS US

Ruth Burgess

THE FEAST OF THE
TRANSFIGURATION

OPENING AND CLOSING RESPONSES FOR THE FEAST OF THE TRANSFIGURATION

Dan 7:9–10,13–14; Ps 97; 2 Pet 1:16–19;
Year A: Mt 17:1–9;
Year B: Mk 9:2–10;
Year C: Lk 9:28–36

Creativity and light
belong to God
LET ALL THE EARTH REJOICE

Justice and glory
belong to God
LET ALL THE EARTH REJOICE

Wisdom and wonder
belong to God
LET ALL THE EARTH REJOICE

> When we get it amazingly wrong
> GOD LOVES US
>
> When we get it superbly right
> GOD LOVES US
>
> When we have no idea at all what is happening
> GOD LOVES US
>
> When we walk with God
> WE DO NOT NEED TO BE AFRAID

JESUS SAID: I AM THE LIGHT OF THE WORLD.
Listen to him and walk in his way.

JESUS SAID: STAND UP AND DON'T BE AFRAID.
Listen to him and walk in his way.

JESUS SAID: YOU ARE MY FRIENDS.
Listen to him and walk in his way.

JESUS SAID: I AM ALWAYS WITH YOU.
Listen to him and walk in his way. AMEN

Star-maker God
YOU ASTOUND US

Transfigured Jesus
YOU DAZZLE US

Life-giving Spirit
YOU BLOW OUR MINDS

You are out of this world
YOU ARE HERE IN OUR LIVES

When we walk with you in wonder
HOLD OUR HANDS

When we walk with you through darkness
HOLD OUR HANDS

When we walk with you in justice
HOLD OUR HANDS

When we walk with you to glory
HOLD OUR HANDS AND BRING US SAFELY HOME

Aware of your glory
TAKE US DOWN THE MOUNTAIN

With love in our lives
TAKE US DOWN THE MOUNTAIN

To our homes and streets
TAKE US DOWN THE MOUNTAIN

Stand us firm on our feet
AND WALK WITH US IN LOVE

Ruth Burgess

THEY SAW HIS GLORY

They saw his glory.
It was him, the carpenter, the teacher,
the one they followed, the one they knew.
Yet it was more than him, and more than the one they knew.
His face was changed.
His clothes shone lightning bright.
He walked and talked with Moses and Elijah,
law-bringer and prophet, heroes of their faith.
And then they heard God speak:
'This is my son, whom I have chosen,
listen to him.'

God sees our glory.
It is me and you. The carpenter, the teacher,
the carer, plumber, clerk. The me and you we know.
Yet we are more than that.
He sees his own creation,
he knows what we can be,
changed and lightning bright.
As we walk with Jesus, do his work, and follow in his way,
we too may hear God speak:
'This is my son, my daughter, whom I have chosen.
Come, share my glory.'

David Lemmon

EVER-CHANGING GOD

(A prayer for transfiguration)

Ever-changing God,
sometimes we plod on,
head down
watching our feet
missing the glimpses of glory.

Ever-changing God,
breaking through into the mundane greyness of our lives
to make all things new,

lift up our eyes to see your glory:
in the taken-for-granted intimacy of human loving,
in the persistent courage of day-to-day struggle,
in the renewal of green growth after winter,
in the new insight that stretches our imagination.

Lift up our eyes
to see the wonder and mystery of your presence
beckoning through the everyday glimpses of grace.
Amen

Jan Berry

Prayer inspired by a phrase from Kathy Galloway.

A PRAYER OF CONFESSION

Father
you are the source of all time.
Yet it neither contains nor constrains you.

We who are time-bound
confess
that often we do not take the time,
or make the time
to enter into your great stillness
and gaze on you.

silence

Forgive us
for all those times
when the restless pursuit of the next thing
has distracted and deflected us
from spending time with you.

silence

Help us to escape the bondage of busyness
and find those moments
of intersection with eternity,
when your time and our time come together
and we can grow in our awareness of you
and of your purposes.

We ask this in the name of Christ –
the one who came into the world
to make visible the Time of God. Amen

Pat Bennett

JAMES AND THE GIANT CLOUD

Peter wanted to build three booths.
He gets a very bad press for that,
but people don't have a clue what it was like.

I haven't had the words to explain it to them, not really.

Prayer has never been so real,

so mind-blowing,
so terrifying!

We were pretty exhausted by the time it happened
but wow – the brightness –
the dazzling, radiant brightness of Jesus –
shocked us into alertness.
And there was Moses
and Elijah!
And we could hear them!

When Peter suggested we enshrine the moment I was totally up for it –
this was more awesome than anything I had experienced –
and life with Jesus had been very miraculous!
Afterwards Peter told me he didn't really know what he was saying,
but he was right –
we had to do something for these giants of the faith,
we had to make a gesture – offer something,
and Pete's always the man for action – diving in feet first!

But the cloud shrouded us
and the voice stopped us in our tracks.
I was terrified.

Afterwards we were still for a long time
and Jesus said we needed to stay put for a while.
None of us argued, we were literally awestruck.

So we waited there, all night,
and we began to grasp something of what we'd seen
and what we'd heard,
as we quietly pondered it all with Jesus.

John summed it up for the three of us
when he said that he was glad we'd stayed up there.
He said something about
needing to stick with the moment –
to make sense of it –

Jesus knew what he was doing
when he kept us up there till morning.
I know the three of us learned a lot about ourselves,
and I know we were better prepared for what was ahead of us.

Alison Adam

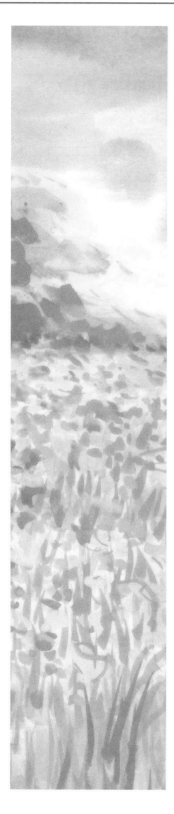

CHRIST TRANSFIGURED

(Tune: St Patrick)

Up from the river's edge you rise
as heaven breaks open to your sight
and earthbound dove descending flies,
announcing that the time is right.
The time is right for you to show
the place where love and glory meet,
in your own person, bending low,
by lakeside cool and sweaty street.

Among the wedding guests you stand
while common folk together throng
and greetings pass from hand to hand
as young and old make merry song.
When water sparkles into wine,
so soon assumes a deeper hue,
this family celebration fine
your love and glory brings to view.

Up to the mountaintop you climb
with closest friends who still are blind,
then in an instant, all sublime,
you open eyes and blow our mind.
With shining white and dazzling light
as love and power conjoin, unite,
transfigured Christ, you bring to sight
glory to banish doubt's dark night.

High on the skull's dark hill you hang
while day is darkened all around,
as flesh is torn, as hammers clang
and foul mouths spew out mocking sound.
But now is love's great victory won,
transfiguration's here complete,
your glory, brighter than the sun,
to life eternal guides our feet.

Within your people now and here,
among your people everywhere,
Jesus your living love make clear,
Jesus your glory now declare.

Open our eyes that we may see
how love and glory endless be
in God's design of unity
where all earth's children shall be free.

Leith Fisher

GOD OF THE ORDINARY

(A prayer of adoration for Transfiguration Day)

God of the ordinary,
we praise you.

You take the drabness of our thoughts,
and brighten them into vivid imagination.

You take our everyday lives,
and transform them into holy, precious moments.

You take our meagre offerings
and multiply them into an abundance of delight.

Extraordinary God,
you light up our thoughts, our lives, our selves
with the wonder of your call. We praise you.
Amen

Jan Berry

TWO BLESSINGS FOR THE FEAST OF THE TRANSFIGURATION

May Jesus the morning star rise in your minds.
May Jesus the morning star rise in your hearts.
May Jesus the morning star rise in your lives.
And may God the light-maker,
Jesus the morning star,
and the Holy Spirit of fire and glory
bless you this day
and every day. AMEN

May we listen to God in creation's beauty and wonder.
May we listen to Jesus in the words that are recorded.
May we listen to the Holy Spirit speaking to us in our world.
And may God bless us with hope and courage
all our nights and days. AMEN

Ruth Burgess

SOURCES AND ACKNOWLEDGEMENTS

'A genderless Trinity' – Words from the song 'Enemy of Apathy' by John L. Bell and Graham Maule, *Enemy of Apathy*, Wild Goose Publications, 1988. Used by permission of the Wild Goose Resource Group, © Wild Goose Resource Group.

The fruit – 'The Fruit' was a runner-up in the International Manchester Cathedral Poetry Competition. Used by permission of Rachel Mann.

'The crown of your creation' – First published in *Sex as Gift*, Ian M Fraser, SCM Press, 1967. Used by permission of Ian M Fraser and SCM/Canterbury Press.

'Behold the Lamb of God (Exodus 12:1–14)' – by Jan Berry, originally published in *URC Prayer Handbook 1998–1999*. Used by permission of Jan Berry, © Jan Berry.

'Breadmaking God' – by Jan Berry, originally published in *URC Prayer Handbook 1998– 1999*. Used by permission of Jan Berry, © Jan Berry.

'Come and see (Andrew remembers)' – by Mary Hanrahan, first published in *Areopagus* magazine. Used by permission of Mary Hanrahan.

'On his way (Luke 4:16–30)' – by Jan Sutch Pickard, from *Imaginary Conversations: Dialogues for Use in Worship and Bible Study*, Methodist Church Overseas Division, 1989/90 © Jan Sutch Pickard. Used by permission of Jan Sutch Pickard.

'O Jesus he spak not a word' – Words by Ian M Fraser, music (Rough encounter) by Ian M Fraser, arranged by Donald Rennie. Words and music © 1994 Stainer & Bell Ltd, 23 Gruneisen Road, London N3 IDZ www.stainer.co.uk. Used by permission of Stainer & Bell.

At the wedding of Jairus's daughter – by Mary Hanrahan, first published in *Alive Now*, July/August 2002 (Nashville, Tennessee). Copyright 2002 by The Upper Room. Used by permission of the publisher and Mary Hanrahan.

'Listen to me (Mark 7:31–37)' – by Ruth Burgess, first written for CTBI. © Ruth Burgess.

'Syrophoenician woman' – by Mary Hanrahan, first published in *Spirituality*. Used by permission of Mary Hanrahan.

'A right relationship' – by Kathy Galloway, first published in *Coracle*, the magazine of the Iona Community www.iona.org.uk

'We know fine well' – by Erik Cramb, extract from *Fallen to Mediocrity: Called to Excellence, an Affirmation of the Spirit of Community in Britain*, Erik Cramb, Wild Goose Publications, 1991.

'Fathers' – by Eleanor Nesbitt, from *Turn but a Stone*, Norwich: Hilton House. Used by permission of Eleanor Nesbitt, © Eleanor Nesbitt.

'The shed' – by Rachel Shepton, first published in *The Flow ... Poetry from Camas*, Rachel McCann (ed.).

'Iona dance' – by Alix Brown, first published in *Coracle*, the magazine of the Iona Community www.iona.org.uk.

'Empty church, West Sutherland' – by Robert Davidson, first published in *Coracle*, the magazine of the Iona Community www.iona.org.uk

'The promised presence (Family group meeting at Connel)' – by Rob Walker, first published in *Coracle*, the magazine of the Iona Community www.iona.org.uk

'We appeal to you: a biblical reflection on 1 Thessalonians' – by Ruth Burgess, first Published by CTBI, 2007. © Ruth Burgess.

'Teach us, Lord Christ, to pray' – words by Ian M Fraser, music (Cults East) by Donald Rennie. Words and music © 1994 Stainer & Bell Ltd, 23 Gruneisen Road, London N3 IDZ www.stainer.co.uk. Used by permission of Stainer & Bell.

'The cost of forgiveness' – by Jan Berry, originally published in *URC Prayer Handbook 1998–1999*. Used by permission of Jan Berry, © Jan Berry.

'The church is sent that it be spent' – words by Ian M Fraser, music (Cammock House) by Donald Rennie. Words and music © 1994 Stainer & Bell Ltd, 23 Gruneisen Road, London N3 IDZ www.stainer.co.uk. Used by permission of Stainer & Bell.

'A solemn blessing' – by Ruth Burgess, first Published by CTBI. © Ruth Burgess.

'A dangerous idea' – by Stuart Barrie, first published in *Coracle*, the magazine of the Iona Community www.iona.org.uk

'Speak to me' – by Marlene Finlayson, first published in *Coracle*, the magazine of the Iona Community www.iona.org.uk

'Storymaking God' – by Jan Berry, first published in *Coracle*, the magazine of the Iona Community www.iona.org.uk

Ever-changing God – by Jan Berry, originally published in *URC Prayer Handbook 1998–1999*. Used by permission of Jan Berry, © Jan Berry.

CONTRIBUTORS

Alison Adam is a member of the Iona Community who works freelance in music and liturgy.

Hilary Allen – 'I work as a doctor and volunteer counsellor. With this background, my writing reflects our struggles and journey in faith.'

Stuart Barrie – 'Engineer, janitor to two dogs, and one wife. Domiciled in East Kilbride, Glasgow.'

Elizabeth Baxter is Executive Director of Holy Rood House, Centre for Health and Pastoral Care, in Thirsk, North Yorkshire, and The Centre for the Study of Theology and Health. As a priest and counsellor she enjoys accompanying people on their therapeutic and spiritual journeys and her liturgy springs from these experiences.

Pat Bennett is PhD student and an associate member of the Iona Community. She has been writing liturgies, prayers and hymns since her first visit to Iona in 1996.

Jan Berry is a minister of the United Reformed Church and teaches practical theology at Luther King House in Manchester, with a particular interest in feminist liturgy and ritual. She lives with her partner, their two cats and a dog, and enjoys walking, dancing and detective stories.

Cally Booker lives, works, weaves and worships in Dundee. She contributes to the liturgy at St Paul's Episcopal Cathedral and gets over-excited about using all the senses in prayer.

Ruth Bowen is a friend of the Iona Community. She lives and works, as a teacher, in the Orkney Islands. She loves the Islands, woolcraft, gardening and people. She believes in a ministry of prayer, healing and reconciliation.

Alix Brown is a psychotherapist working with young people and a member of the Iona Community. She lives in Shropshire with her partner Polly and various animals.

Graeme Brown is a minister of the Church of Scotland and a member of the Iona Community.

Julia Brown works in Durham where she lives with her husband and three children. Writing poetry is one of the ways in which she is exploring her latent creativity.

David J. M. Coleman is a member of the Iona Community, a URC minister and a digital artist, working in Brighthelm Church, Brighton.

Roddy Cowie is a research psychologist who works on 'humanising computing' (getting computers to communicate in ways that suit human beings rather than expecting humans to communicate in ways that suit the computers). He is a lay reader in Belfast, and an Iona Community associate member, who started coming to Iona before he was born, and has been back most years since.

Erik Cramb is a retired Industrial Chaplain living in Dundee. He has been a member of the Iona Community since 1972.

da Noust are part of the ecumenical L'Arche Edinburgh community that welcomes people with learning difficulties, employed assistants and volunteers to a shared life founded on the values of simplicity, mutual faithfulness and accountability (www.larche.org.uk). Further community resources for shared prayer – songs, carols, texts – can be accessed via da_noust@yahoo.co.uk

Ed Daub is an associate of the Iona Community, a retired Presbyterian minister (who served the United Church of Christ in Japan, 1951–1963, as a Fraternal Worker), and Professor Emeritus at the University of Wisconsin-Madison, where he initiated the pro-gramme in technical Japanese.

Robert Davidson is a writer, editor and publisher based in the Scottish Highlands.

John Davies is a member of the Iona Community in Liverpool who writes on the theme of 'Heaven in the ordinary' at www.johndavies.org

Simon de Voil works in the MacLeod Centre, gardening, welcoming and including guests (and anyone else) into the life of the community on Iona. He's dedicated to making church more down to earth and emotionally relevant, especially for people who find it boring.

Judy Dinnen – 'I am an associate of the Iona Community. As a curate in the beautiful South Herefordshire valleys, I appreciate the resources in Wild Goose Publications.'

Carol Dixon was born and brought up in Alnwick, Northumberland and is a lay preacher in the United Reformed Church. She is a Friend of St Cuthbert's, Holy Island. She enjoys writing Northumbrian songs, and her hymns have been published in *All Year Round*, *Songs for the New Millennium*, *Worship Live*, and the Church of Scotland Hymnbook. Carol is a wife and mother with a daughter and twin sons and enjoys being a grandmother.

Marlene Finlayson – 'For the past fifteen years, I have been living on the Orkney Main-land, where I am an Early Years teacher. I am a founder member of the Orkney Inter-faith group.'

Leith Fisher retired in 2006 after ministries in Falkirk, Glasgow Calton and Wellington. Leith is a hymn writer and the author of *Will You Follow Me?: Exploring the Gospel of Mark*, and *The Widening Road – from Bethlehem to Emmaus: Exploring the Gospel of Luke*

(Scottish Christian Press). He is married to Nonie and they have five grown-up children. Leith has been a member of the Iona Community since 1966.

Brian Ford – 'I was a biology teacher. Now I am retired I am enjoying having a little more time to write poems, particularly those which look at biblical stories from different points of view.'

Andrew Foster is an engineer living in Ontario, Canada, a friend of the Iona Community, an elder in The Presbyterian Church in Canada, a frequent visitor to Iona and a contributor to some of Ruth Burgess's previous books.

David Fox was born in Newbridge, Monmouthshire. He studied chemistry in University College London and taught for a while in Reading. Now a member of the United Reformed Church serving in Penarth, he has contributed to a number of ecumenical publications for CTBI and Cytun and has had hymns published in a number of collections both at home and overseas.

Ian M Fraser – 'What is important about my life is that Margaret married me, and the family is 3 children, 9 grandchildren and (so far) 4 great-grandchildren. I have been a member of the Iona Community since 1941.'

Alma Fritchley spends her days looking after Her Majesty's tax affairs and her spare time writing prose, poems and novels! She lives with her dog, two cats and her Civil Partner in the leafy loveliness that is the suburbs of Manchester.

Kathy Galloway is the current leader of the Iona Community.

Terry Garley has served as the Ecumenical Development Officer for Churches Together in Lancashire since August 2000 and retires in August 2008 after more than twenty-five years of working in the ecumenical movement in a professional capacity. The Anglican partner of an Anglican-Methodist marriage, she served on the group which produced an Anglican-Methodist Covenant, signed on 1 November 2003 in the presence of Her Majesty the Queen; during the 1990's Terry was Deputy Moderator (1990–1995) and Moderator (1995–1999) of the Churches Together in England Forum.

Tom Gordon is a member of the Iona Community. He is the author of *A Need for Living: Signposts on the Journey of Life and Beyond* and *New Journeys Now Begin: Learning on the Path of Grief and Loss* (Wild Goose Publications).

Alison Gray is from Kilsyth in Scotland, but lives in Tokyo, Japan. When not raising her young son, she organises a feminist theology group. Other hobbies include writing and promoting fair trade and the trade justice movement in Japan. She is a member of the Iona Community.

Julie Greenan is a member of All Hallows Church, Hyde Park, Leeds. Her writing has been inspired by the people of this community.

Liz Gregory-Smith is married with two adult sons. She enjoys writing, alongside her responsibilities as a reader in the village Anglican church.

David Hamflett is a Methodist minister and a friend of the Iona Community working in the north of England, and has a special interest in compiling and composing liturgies. He sings traditional folk songs and plays the guitar and the bodhrán.

Mary Hanrahan – 'I am a primary schoolteacher in the east end of Glasgow and an active member of St Paul the Apostle Roman Catholic Church in Shettleston. My poetry has been published in various small press magazines.'

Margaret Harvey is a founder member of the Coleg y Groes Community and helps to run the Coleg y Groes Retreat House in Corwen, North Wales (www.colegygroes. co.uk). She is a native of Wales and a Church in Wales priest.

Pam Hathorn is now retired from her career as a special needs teacher. She wonders how she will manage to fit in everything that still remains to be seen, heard and written!

Frances Hawkey – 'I am an associate member of the Iona Community and worked at the Abbey as Housekeeper for a year. I reached the watershed of seventy in January this year (2008), which set me thinking a good deal! (But it's actually OK!)'

Martin Hayden is a Quaker, a tennis player, an amateur pianist, and a writer, and has lived in Suffolk since 1982.

Judith Jessop is a Methodist minister currently working in Sheffield, a single parent caring for her two teenage children, and an associate member of the Iona Community.

Karen Jobson is a Methodist minister with particular interests in spirituality and the arts. She hates and loves the Church in equal measures.

Elizabeth Kime is a worship leader in her local church. She lives in County Durham with her husband and two sons.

Anne Lawson is Vicar of Haslington and Crewe Green in Cheshire. Hindered rather than helped by Nimrod, her cuddly ginger cat, she writes poetry in her spare time.

David Lemmon is a retired youth worker and youth work trainer, living in Beckenham, Kent. He is a Methodist Local Preacher and a friend of the Iona Community.

Kareen Lowther lives in Walsall in the West Midlands and is a Church of England Team Vicar with responsibility for Holy Ascension Church, Bloxwich. She has begun experimenting with writing poetry and prose for use in worship over the last few years, and this is the first time her work has been published.

Murdoch MacKenzie is a member of the Iona Community and lives in retirement in Argyll. He has worked in India and is still involved in a variety of ways in the ecumenical movement.

Rachel Mann is an Anglican priest based in south Manchester. Her poetry, liturgical and theological writing has appeared in numerous publications, including several Wild Goose anthologies. One day she hopes to be responsible enough to own a pet.

Lesley Mitchinson is an Edinburgh University graduate, and taught English before marrying a Scottish Infantry officer and leading a stimulating nomadic life. Now widowed, she lives near Glasgow and has two sons.

Carolyn Morris is an ex-teacher who now creates her own original books. She appreciates art, crafts and books, and shares with A. Wainwright a love of walking and a stumbling relationship with the human race.

Rosie Morton is currently Assistant Curate at St Mary's Parish Handsworth in Birmingham Diocese, which is a good and interesting place to grow in ministry. She likes to read and write poetry, hill walk, cook and have fun with friends and family.

Eleanor Nesbitt writes limericks and is Professor in Religions and Education at the University of Warwick. Her (serious) publications include *Intercultural Education: Ethnographic and Religious Approaches* (2004, Sussex Academic Press) and *Sikhism: A Very Short Introduction* (2005, Oxford University Press).

Mary Palmer has an MA in creative writing; her first book *Iona*, a story told through poems, prose and images, came out in April. She also performs her work and teaches creative writing.

Neil Paynter has been an English teacher to immigrants to Canada, a nurse's aide, a night shelter worker, a 'counsellor', a community worker, a farm labourer, a fruit picker, a bookseller, a hospital cleaner, a stand-up comedian, a musician, an editorial assistant. He is an editor with Wild Goose Publications and the Editor of *Coracle*, the magazine of the Iona Community www.iona.org.uk

Chris Polhill is a member of the Iona Community and the author of *Eggs & Ashes* (with Ruth Burgess) and *A Pilgrim's Guide to Iona Abbey* (Wild Goose Publications). She is a priest in the Church of England.

John Polhill took early retirement from his career as an IT systems consultant to design and build a series of small gardens that portray themes about care for the environment and the Christian spiritual journey.

Jan Sutch Pickard is a member of the Iona Community, a writer, a storyteller and a Methodist preacher. She is the author of *Between High and Low Water: Sojourner Songs;*

Out of Iona: Words from a Crossroads of the World; *Advent Readings from Iona* (with Brian Woodcock); and *Dandelions and Thistles* (Wild Goose Publications).

Aniko Schuetz is currently the Sacristan of Iona Abbey. She enjoys music, nature, sailing, yoga and being creative in any way.

Alizon Sharun has a background in English language and literature. She is a singer and community musician, costume designer, gardener, seamstress and transatlantic way-farer, living mostly in Canada. She is an associate of the Iona Community and a lover of ordinary time.

Rachel Shepton spent her first 30 years of life in England and Scotland, and many happy summers on Iona and Mull. She now lives with her husband and two small girls on a rural property close to Darwin in the tropical north of Australia.

Thom M Shuman, poet/pastor in the States, is author of *The Jesse Tree* (Wild Goose Publications) and a contributor to other Iona resources.

Josie Smith has been a teacher, a freelance radio and TV broadcaster, a Methodist preacher, and worked for 13 years on the staff of the Methodist headquarters. She is now actively retired in Sheffield.

Carolyn Smyth – a member of the Iona Community, living in Glasgow, who, through God's grace, finds the ambiguity and beauty of grey more life-giving than the certainty of white and black; still scary though!

Simon Taylor is a Baptist minister living on Dartmoor, who uses images from the world around us in his prayers and liturgies. He works for Churches Together in Devon and is also Free Church minister at Christ Church in Estover, an ecumenical partnership in North Plymouth.

Rob Walker is a building conservation officer in Herefordshire. He was a member of the Iona Resident Group 2002–2004.

Pamela Whyman is a retired teacher, who has recently been commissioned by the Bishop of Birmingham with others to be part of the Pastoral Care Team for their church. She enjoys music and gardening.

Lynda Wright – After working for eleven years in parish ministry as a deacon for the Church of Scotland and three years at the Abbey as part of the resident group, Lynda is presently based in Fife where for the last fifteen years she has welcomed people to Key House, offering both hospitality and retreats.

INDEX OF AUTHORS

THE IONA COMMUNITY IS:

- An ecumenical movement of men and women from different walks of life and different traditions in the Christian church
- Committed to the gospel of Jesus Christ, and to following where that leads, even into the unknown
- Engaged together, and with people of goodwill across the world, in acting, reflecting and praying for justice, peace and the integrity of creation
- Convinced that the inclusive community we seek must be embodied in the community we practise

Together with our staff, we are responsible for:

- Our islands residential centres of Iona Abbey, the MacLeod Centre on Iona, and Camas Adventure Centre on the Ross of Mull

and in Glasgow:

- The administration of the Community
- Our work with young people
- Our publishing house, Wild Goose Publications
- Our association in the revitalising of worship with the Wild Goose Resource Group

The Iona Community was founded in Glasgow in 1938 by George MacLeod, minister, visionary and prophetic witness for peace, in the context of the poverty and despair of the Depression. Its original task of rebuilding the monastic ruins of Iona Abbey became a sign of hopeful rebuilding of community in Scotland and beyond. Today, we are about 250 members, mostly in Britain, and 1500 associate members, with 1400 friends worldwide. Together and apart, 'we follow the light we have, and pray for more light'.

For information on the Iona Community contact:
The Iona Community, Fourth Floor, Savoy House, 140 Sauchiehall Street,
Glasgow G2 3DH, UK. Phone: 0141 332 6343
e-mail: admin@iona.org.uk; web: www.iona.org.uk

For enquiries about visiting Iona, please contact:
Iona Abbey, Isle of Iona, Argyll PA76 6SN, UK. Phone: 01681 700404
e-mail: ionacomm@iona.org.uk

Wild Goose Publications, the publishing house of the Iona Community established in the Celtic Christian tradition of Saint Columba, produces books, CDs and digital downloads on:

- holistic spirituality
- social justice
- political and peace issues
- healing
- innovative approaches to worship
- song in worship, including the work of the Wild Goose Resource Group
- material for meditation and reflection

For more information:

Wild Goose Publications
Fourth Floor, Savoy House
140 Sauchiehall Street,
Glasgow G2 3DH, UK

Tel. +44 (0)141 332 6292
Fax +44 (0)141 332 1090
e-mail: admin@ionabooks.com

or visit our website at
www.ionabooks.com
for details of all our products and online sales